## Dedication

This book is dedicated to all who have sacrificed in the defense of freedom, in ways both great and small.

# Acknowledgments

I offer my sincere thanks first to Bill Zumwalde, who did a considerable amount of the initial development for this edition and handled many of the screenshots. Bill did an outstanding job and made it possible for us to hit our deadlines with a quality product.

I thank Lisa Thibault, Executive Editor, for her help in managing the book and submissions. I also thank Lori Lyons, the production coordinator for this edition, for her efforts in directing the content and managing the process. I also want to recognize Michael Young, Rebecca Ross, and Marjorie Baer for bringing me this opportunity—and especially to Michael for developing a solid first edition of the book.

I also sincerely appreciate the efforts of Technical Editor David Jung, who did a great job of checking the content and pointing out areas that needed to be clarified and fine-tuned.

# CONTENTS AT A GLANCE

# TABLE OF CONTENTS

**TABLE OF CONTENTS**

# INTRODUCTION

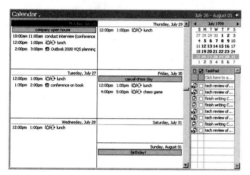

**Figure i.1** Appointments and events stored in the Outlook Calendar folder.

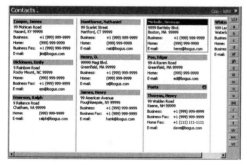

**Figure i.2** Contact information stored in the Outlook Contacts folder.

You can use Microsoft Outlook 2003 to organize and plan your business or personal life, to communicate and share information with people in your company or anywhere on the Internet, and to collaborate with your co-workers on group projects.

Here's a more detailed sampling of what you can do with Outlook:

◆ Send, receive, store, and organize email and fax messages

◆ Keep a calendar of your personal appointments and events, and schedule meetings with other people (**Figure i.1**)

◆ Store names, addresses, and other information on your business and personal contacts (**Figure i.2**)

◆ Quickly send a message to a contact, dial a contact's phone number, or reach a contact in other ways

◆ Keep track of the personal tasks you need to complete, and manage group projects

*continues on next page*

- ◆ Maintain a record of activities or occurrences that take place in your business or personal life, such as receiving an email message, creating a document, or making a phone call

- ◆ Quickly type and store miscellaneous bits of information in electronic "sticky notes" (**Figure i.3**)

- ◆ Share any of your Outlook information with other people on a network

- ◆ Create and manage group schedules to view others' free/busy times

- ◆ Explore Web pages in the Outlook window, without having to run a separate browser program

**Figure i.3** A note stored in the Outlook Notes folder.

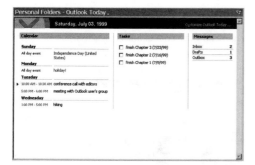

**Figure i.4** Outlook displaying the Outlook Today folder.

*Find page*

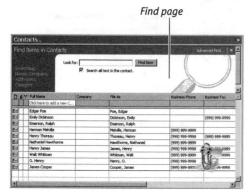

**Figure i.5** The Find page displayed above the information in the opened Outlook folder.

# New Features in Outlook 2003

The original version of Outlook was part of the Microsoft Office 97 suite of applications. Outlook has acquired many new features since then in Outlook 98, Outlook 2000, and Outlook 2002 (this latter version included with Office XP). Outlook 2002 saw several significant changes, and many features are brand new in Outlook 2003, the latest version. The following sections describe many of these new features.

## New features in Outlook 98

- ◆ The **Outlook Today** folder, which displays a Web-style page that gives you an overview of the current information in several commonly used Outlook folders, and lets you quickly manage this information (**Figure i.4**).

- ◆ The **Find page**, a Web-style page that you can display in a separate pane and use to find Outlook items containing specific text (**Figure i.5**).

- ◆ The **Organize page**, a Web-style page that you can display in a separate pane and use to quickly work with Outlook items. For example, you can use this page to create rules for automatically moving or color-coding selected messages (messages from or to a particular person, junk messages, or adult-content messages).

- ◆ Support for the **HTML email** format, which lets you include backgrounds, graphics, and other Web-page content in your email messages. You can use predesigned **stationery** to get a head start in creating an attractive HTML email message for a specific purpose (such as a party invitation or an announcement).

*continues on next page*

NEW FEATURES IN OUTLOOK 2003

◆ Support for standard **Internet email** protocols so that you can use Outlook with a wider variety of email services (SMTP, POP3, and IMAP4).

◆ An enhanced **Preview pane** that lets you view the entire contents of an email message.

◆ Automatic saving of messages while you compose them, in the **Drafts** folder.

◆ The use of **Internet directory (LDAP)** services for verifying or finding people's email addresses.

### New features in Outlook 2000

◆ **Folder home pages**, which let you display Web-style information in any Outlook folder.

◆ **Custom menus and toolbars**, which show only the commands you use most frequently.

◆ **Personal distribution lists**, which you can store in your Contacts folder and use to quickly send messages to entire groups of people.

◆ The **Find A Contact** list box on the Standard toolbar, which lets you rapidly find a contact wherever you are in Outlook (**Figure i.6**).

◆ Viewing **Web pages** right in the Outlook window (**Figure i.7**), using the new **Favorites menu** or **Web-page shortcuts** in the Outlook Bar.

**Figure i.6** The Find A Contact list box.

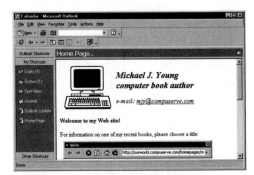

**Figure i.7** A Web page displayed within the Outlook window.

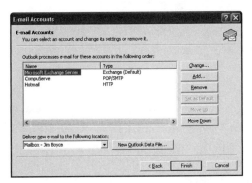

**Figure i.8** Unified mode to support all types of accounts in one profile.

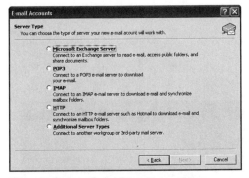

**Figure i.9** Support for additional account types.

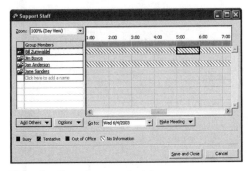

**Figure i.10** Named group schedules.

## New features in Outlook 2002

◆ **Unified mode** (continued in Outlook 2003), which eliminates the Corporate/ Workgroup and Internet Only modes in previous versions, enabling you to work with all types of accounts in a single profile (**Figure i.8**).

◆ **Improved and expanded rules** for organizing and processing messages.

◆ Integration of **Instant Messaging** (IM) in Outlook to let you tell at a glance if a contact or message sender is online.

◆ **Attachment blocking** and **extended virus protection** to help prevent virus infections and worm-based email propagation.

◆ **Safe mode startup** to enable Outlook to start when it would otherwise fail.

◆ **Better support** for different email accounts including **IMAP** and **HTTP** (**Figure i.9**).

◆ **Expansion of Remote Mail** features to support account types other than Exchange Server.

◆ **Support for named group schedules**, which enable you to view others' free/busy times without creating an appointment (**Figure i.10**).

## New features in Outlook 2003

◆ A **streamlined interface** for Outlook to provide better ease-of-use (**Figure i.11**).

◆ **Cached Exchange mode**, which creates a local copy of your Exchange Server mailbox, making your mailbox available even when the server is not available. Outlook handles synchronization with the server automatically.

◆ **Search folders**, which are virtual folders that provide a means for easy filtering of messages. The messages that fit the filter criteria appear as if they are in a separate named folder, simplifying message organization.

Navigation pane

Reading pane

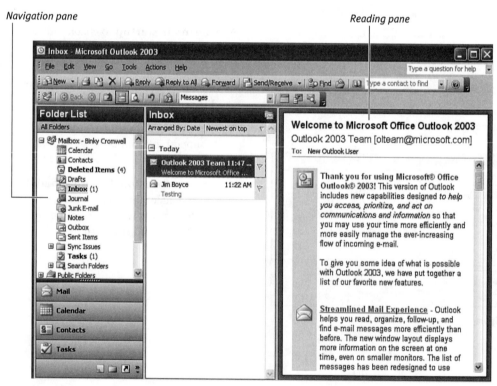

**Figure i.11** An improved user interface.

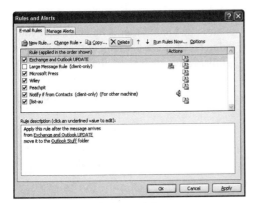

**Figure i.12** Enhanced rules and alerts.

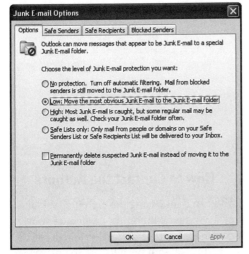

**Figure i.13** Additional features to block junk mail.

◆ A new **Navigation pane** that takes the place of the Outlook Bar in previous versions, and a **Reading pane** that takes the place of the Preview pane.

◆ Improved and **expanded rules for organizing and processing** messages.

◆ **Additional alerts** that notify you when messages arrive. You can create **custom alerts** to receive notification for specific types of messages, such as those from specific senders (**Figure i.12**).

◆ Considerably improved **junk mail filtering** to weed out unwanted messages, and **blocking of Web beacons** (remote image links in messages) that spammers use to identify valid recipients (**Figure i.13**).

◆ Better **integration of Instant Messaging (IM)** in Outlook, with a **Person Names smart tag** that tells you if a contact or message sender is online and provides quick access to IM commands and tasks.

**NEW FEATURES IN OUTLOOK 2003**

# How to Use the Book

As a *Visual QuickStart Guide*, this book is targeted at Outlook users who need a quick introduction to the most important and frequently used features in Outlook. You don't need much experience using Word, but you do need a basic understanding of how to use the mouse and work in Windows.

I recommend that you read the book in the following way:

◆ If you haven't installed Outlook yet, read Chapter 1 for installation instructions and for help in making installation choices. This chapter refers you to Appendix A for instructions on some of the more involved configuration tasks you might need to complete during setup.

◆ Read Chapter 2, especially if you're new to Outlook or Office, to get an overview of Outlook's features and the types of information it manages, and to learn basic Windows and Office skills.

◆ Read through Chapters 3 and 4 to learn the basic Outlook techniques you'll need when you work with almost any of the types of information Outlook manages. Refer back to these chapters as you start to work with the different Outlook folders.

◆ Chapters 5 through 11 cover each of the main types of information that Outlook manages. You can read just those chapters that cover the information types you want to work with, and you can read them in any order.

◆ Read Chapter 12 to learn how to use some of the more advanced features in Outlook, including a handful of features specific to Exchange Server accounts.

◆ Read Chapter 13 if you want to use Outlook to explore Web pages.

◆ Read Chapter 14 if you want to customize Outlook. I recommend, however, that you don't customize Outlook until you've finished working through the other chapters, so your program commands will match those described in the book.

## How to Contact the Authors

You can contact me through my Web site at www.mjyOnline.com. I welcome your comments and feedback. Although my schedule seldom permits me to answer questions that require research, if you have a question that I can answer readily, I'll be happy to share what I know.

At my Web site you'll also find book corrections, reader questions and answers, sources for getting additional help on Outlook and Office, descriptions of some of my other books, and additional information.

To contact Jim Boyce, email boyce_jim@compuserve.com. You'll find additional information about Outlook, Windows, and other topics at Jim's Web site, http://www.boyce.us.

# SETTING UP OUTLOOK 2003

**1**

This chapter shows you how to complete the three main steps for getting Outlook up and running:

◆ **Installing the Outlook software.** Whether you purchased Outlook 2003 as a part of Microsoft Office 2003 or obtained it as a separate product, your first step is to install the Outlook program.

◆ **Running Outlook for the first time.** You can run the Outlook program in several different ways, or you can have it run automatically whenever you start Windows.

◆ **Supplying setup information.** The first time you run Outlook, it prompts you for any setup information that it needs.

## To install Outlook 2003:

1. Run the Setup program on the product CD, following the instructions provided (**Figure 1.1**).

   The Setup program prompts you for the necessary setup information. At one point, it allows you to select the Outlook component that will be installed (**Figure 1.2**).

2. Accept the Typical Install of components.

   *or*

   Select the specific components you want to install by choosing the Custom Install option.

   *or*

   Ideally, if you already have a previous Outlook version installed, use the Upgrade option to configure the installation using your existing Outlook mail accounts (**Figure 1.3**). It will also give you the option to import an existing account from Outlook Express (**Figure 1.4**). If you choose this option, you will then be prompted to import email messages and the address book (**Figure 1.5**).

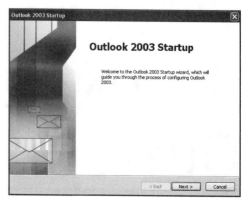

**Figure 1.1** The opening Setup program dialog box.

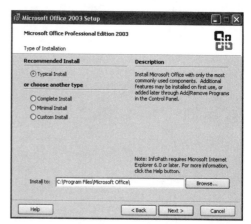

**Figure 1.2** Selecting an installation type.

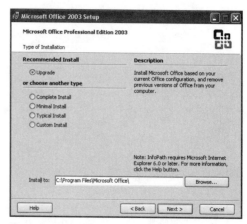

**Figure 1.3** Upgrading an existing Office installation to Office 2003.

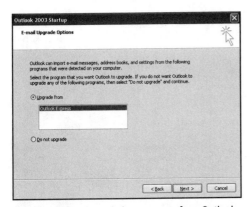

**Figure 1.4** Importing existing accounts from Outlook Express.

**Figure 1.5** You have the option to import existing email and addresses.

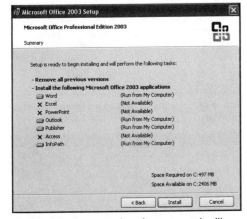

**Figure 1.6** Setup summarizes the programs it will install.

3. Enter the other information that the Setup program requests.

The Setup program will now copy the Outlook software to your hard disk and install Outlook in Windows.

## ✔ Tips

■ Choosing the Typical option installs all Microsoft Office programs to run from My Computer, whereas Minimal leaves Access to be installed upon first use. If you choose Custom installation, installation of Word is recommended so that you can use it as your email editor (**Figure 1.6**).

*continues on next page*

**S**ETTING **U**P **O**UTLOOK **2003**

■ Like the other major Office applications, Outlook includes a set of separate installable components, such as Help, Stationery, and Junk E-mail. Access this by selecting Choose Advanced Customization of Applications (**Figure 1.7**). From there you can select which options you want to install (**Figure 1.8**).

■ I recommend accepting the default set of Outlook components. You will then have everything you need to work with this book. If you later want to add or remove a component, follow the instructions in the section "Adding or Removing Outlook Components" in Appendix A, "Configuring Outlook."

■ In the list of installable Outlook components, those marked with a disk symbol are installed by default. Note that the "1" next to a disk symbol means the component will be installed the first time you use it. The components marked with an "X" are not installed by default.

■ I recommend not checking the box to Delete Installation Files in Setup, as they simplify updates and maintenance (**Figure 1.9**).

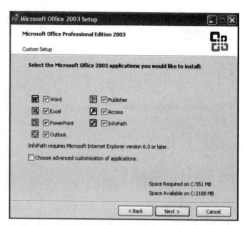

**Figure 1.7** Selecting which programs to install.

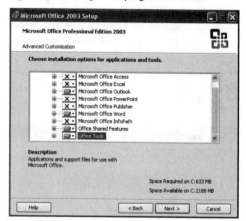

**Figure 1.8** Selecting installation options for individual programs.

**Figure 1.9** Do not check this option if you want to make it easier to add features not installed; check this option if you need to conserve hard disk space.

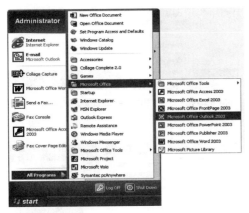

**Figure 1.10** Starting Outlook from the Windows Start menu.

*Click the Launch Microsoft Outlook button*

**Figure 1.11** Starting Outlook from the Quick Launch toolbar.

**Figure 1.12** Enabling the Quick Launch toolbar.

# Running Outlook

After you've finished the Setup program, you can start Outlook at any time. Keep in mind that the first time you run it, you'll probably have to enter some setup information.

## To run Outlook:

◆ Open the Windows Start menu by clicking the Start button on your Windows Taskbar (**Figure 1.10**). Choose Microsoft Outlook from the menu.

*or*

Double-click the Microsoft Outlook icon on your Windows desktop.

*or*

Click the Launch Microsoft Outlook button in the Quick Launch toolbar on the Windows Taskbar (**Figure 1.11**). You may need to enable the Quick Launch toolbar. To do so, right-click the Taskbar and choose Toolbars > Quick Launch. Or, right-click the Taskbar, choose Properties, and check the Show Quick Launch option in the Taskbar and Start menu Properties dialog box (**Figure 1.12**).

## ✔ Tip

■ For instructions on using the mouse and choosing menu commands, see the section "Learning Basic Windows and Office Techniques" in Chapter 2, "Getting Started Using Outlook."

**RUNNING OUTLOOK**

## To have Outlook run automatically every time you start Windows:

1. Right-click the Start menu, and choose Explore (**Figure 1.13**).

2. Browse to \Documents and Settings\ All Users\Start Menu\Programs, and double-click on the Microsoft Office folder. Right-click on the Microsoft Office Outlook 2003 icon and choose Copy (**Figure 1.14**).

3. Browse to the \Documents and Settings\All Users\Start Menu\ Programs\Startup folder. Right-click on the Startup folder, and choose Paste.

### ✔ Tips

- For instructions on working with the mouse, menus, and dialog boxes, see the section "Learning Basic Windows and Office Techniques" in Chapter 2.

- If you can't find the Outlook shortcut in \Documents and Settings\All Users\Start Menu\Programs\Microsoft Office folder, Office might have been installed to a different folder. Click Start > Search and search the hard disk for Outlook.exe to locate the correct folder.

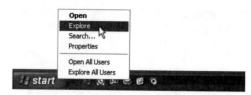

**Figure 1.13** Opening the Start menu in Windows Explorer.

**Figure 1.14** Copying the Outlook shortcut to the Clipboard.

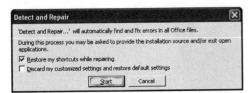

**Figure 1.15** The Detect and Repair command will fix any errors that it finds in the Outlook program files.

# Supplying Setup Information

The first time you run Outlook, it will generally display a series of wizard dialog boxes to prompt you for any required setup information. The particular setup dialog boxes you see—if you see any—depend upon the email software you have previously installed on your computer, the way you've configured this software, and the choices you make as you begin supplying information.

### ✔ Tips

- The following instructions in this chapter describe the basic wizard dialog boxes that you might need to fill in during Outlook setup. Keep in mind that you might see all or none of these, depending on your particular situation.

- Appendix A provides instructions for some of the more involved configuration tasks you might need to complete during Outlook setup. The following instructions provide specific references to Appendix A where necessary.

- Outlook gathers only the minimal setup information required to get you started using the program and often makes choices for you. Keep in mind, however, that you can later change any configuration option by following the instructions given in Appendix A.

- If, after you set up and run Outlook, you encounter a problem that seems to be a program defect, choose the Detect and Repair command on the Help menu. This command fixes any errors that it finds in the Outlook program files (**Figure 1.15**).

# The Outlook Startup Wizard

If you performed an upgrade of a previous version of Outlook with Outlook 2003, Outlook automatically incorporates your previous profiles and accounts and starts up just as it did for your previous installation. You do not need to configure accounts or take any other steps to start using Outlook unless you now want to add other accounts. If that's the case, you are ready to move onto Chapter 2.

If you haven't previously installed Outlook 2003 on your computer, or it finds no Outlook profiles or accounts from a previous installation, Outlook begins by running the Outlook Startup Wizard the first time you start the program. The first dialog box is shown in **Figure 1.16**.

## To complete the Account Configuration dialog box:

1.  Click Next in the Outlook Startup Wizard to display the Account Configuration dialog box (**Figure 1.17**), select Yes, and click the Next button.

2.  Choose one of the five email options shown in **Figure 1.18**.

    For help in making your choice, see the following tips and, if necessary, consult with your email service provider or your corporate network administrator.

3.  Click the Next button.

4.  Follow the remaining prompts to configure the settings for the account. See Appendix A for details on setting up specific types of email accounts in Outlook.

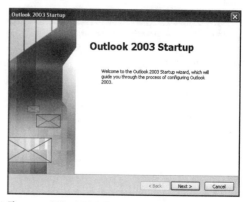

**Figure 1.16** The initial Startup Wizard dialog box.

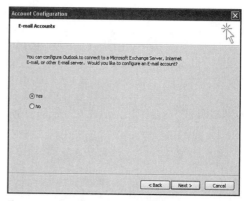

**Figure 1.17** Outlook prompts you to add an email account.

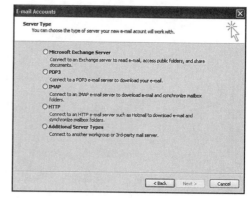

**Figure 1.18** Choose the type of account to add.

## ✔ Tips

■ Select POP3 or IMAP if your email service uses standard Internet protocols (SMTP for outgoing email and either POP3 or IMAP for incoming email).

■ Select Microsoft Exchange Server if you are accessing an Exchange Server account on your network.

■ Select the HTTP option if you want to access a Web-based mail account, such as Hotmail.

■ Click No at the first Account Configuration dialog box if you don't want to use Outlook to manage email.

■ If you're connected to a Microsoft Exchange Server network, you can use the Account Configuration Wizard to set up Exchange Server as your email service. In addition to email, Exchange Server adds many workgroup features to Outlook—for example, sharing information, scheduling meetings, and managing group projects.

■ You can add or remove accounts at any time in Outlook. Just choose Tools > E-mail Accounts to start the E-mail Accounts Wizard.

THE OUTLOOK STARTUP WIZARD

# The E-mail Upgrade Options Dialog Box

If you currently have another email program installed on your computer, Outlook might be able to "upgrade" it. In other words, it might be able to import the email messages, address book, and settings from that program, so you can continue to use your same email service and setup in Outlook without interruption.

If the Outlook 2003 Startup Wizard detects the presence of a program that it can upgrade (such as Qualcomm Eudora, Lotus Organizer, Microsoft Outlook Express, and other popular email programs), it displays the Microsoft Office Outlook dialog box shown in **Figure 1.19**. If you click Yes, the Startup Wizard displays the E-mail Upgrade Options dialog box (**Figure 1.20**).

## To complete the E-mail Upgrade Options dialog box:

1. Click the name of an email program to upgrade it (**Figure 1.20**).

   When you click Next, Outlook displays additional dialog boxes, such as the ones shown in **Figure 1.21** and **Figure 1.22**, that allow you to confirm the settings it is importing. When you complete this wizard, you're done with this chapter and you can go directly to Chapter 2. (If you later want to change your email setup, follow the instructions in Appendix A.)

   *or*

   Click Do Not Upgrade (**Figure 1.20**) if you don't want to upgrade an existing email program.

**Figure 1.19** Outlook can import from your current email program.

**Figure 1.20** Converting from an existing email account.

**Figure 1.21** Entering the name for the account.

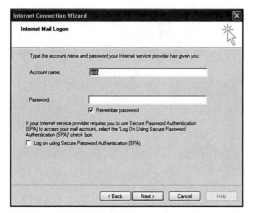

**Figure 1.22** Entering the account name and password.

**Figure 1.23**
Getting help on converting
from Lotus cc:Mail.

If you make this choice and click Next, the wizard will display the Account Configuration dialog box shown earlier in **Figure 1.17**. Follow the steps in the section "To complete the Account Configuration dialog box" earlier in this chapter to add an email account, or click No if you do not want to add an account. Later, if you wish, you can import messages, addresses, and settings from your old email program by following the instructions in "Importing Settings or Data from Another EMail Program" in Appendix A.

**2.** Click the Next button and follow any remaining prompts to complete the Startup Wizard.

## ✔ Tips

- If you're switching from another email or scheduling program to Outlook, you might find useful conversion information in Outlook's Help documents. After installing Outlook, type the name of your previous program (for example, Lotus or Schedule+) into the Help text box, which is labeled Type a Question for Help, or type the name in the Office Assistant. Click the Search button (**Figure 1.23**).

- For instructions on using the Office Assistant, see the section "Consulting the Assistant" in Chapter 2.

# GETTING STARTED USING OUTLOOK

In this chapter, you'll get started using Outlook by learning the following:

◆ The various parts of the Outlook window and the way Outlook organizes information.

◆ How to perform basic Windows and Office techniques:
   ▲ Using the mouse
   ▲ Using menus, toolbars, and keyboard commands
   ▲ Working with dialog boxes
   ▲ Getting help

◆ How to navigate through Outlook and open folders containing different kinds of information.

## ✔ Tip

■ The "Running Outlook" section in Chapter 1, "Setting Up Outlook 2003," described the different ways to start Outlook.

# The Outlook Window

**Figure 2.1** shows the Outlook window as it might appear when you first start the program.

## ✔ Tips

- Your initial Outlook window might look different from the one shown in **Figure 2.1**, depending on the way you set up Outlook or the way you configured a previous version of Outlook. For example, the Navigation Pane might contain different shortcuts, the set of Outlook folders might vary, and your window might display different toolbars. Later in the book, you'll learn how to modify all of these features.

- You can show or hide the status bar at the bottom of the Outlook window by choosing the Status Bar command on the View menu. (See "To choose a menu command," later in the chapter.)

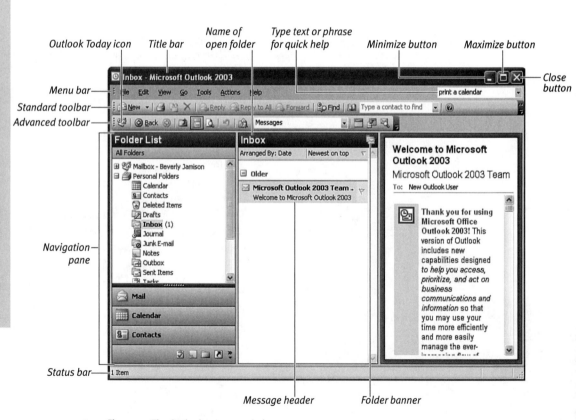

Figure 2.1 The Outlook program window.

# How Outlook Is Organized

The information Outlook manages is stored within a set of Outlook folders. Each Outlook folder stores, displays, and manages a particular type of information—for example, messages, appointments, names and addresses, tasks, or notes. The following are the default folders that Outlook initially creates for you and the types of information that each folder contains:

◆ **Outlook Today** displays a Web-style page that provides an overview of the current information in commonly used Outlook folders and lets you quickly manage this information.

◆ **Inbox** receives your incoming email and fax messages.

◆ **Drafts** stores the messages you are composing, before you send them.

◆ **Outbox** temporarily holds the messages you have sent until they can be transmitted to the recipients.

◆ **Sent Items** keeps a copy of all messages you have sent.

◆ **Calendar** handles appointments, events, and meetings.

◆ **Contacts** manages information on your friends and business associates.

◆ **Tasks** keeps a list of the jobs you or others need to complete.

◆ **Notes** stores miscellaneous bits of information that you jot down.

◆ **Journal** maintains a record of various types of events, such as sending an email message, accessing an Office file, or making a phone call.

◆ **Deleted Items** temporarily holds the Outlook items you've removed until they are permanently deleted.

*continues on next page*

How Outlook Is Organized

A particular piece of information contained in an Outlook folder is called an Outlook item—for example, a message in the Inbox folder, an appointment in the Calendar folder, a pending task in the Tasks folder, or a note in the Notes folder.

Outlook also lets you access the files on your local or network disks. The integrated file management feature of Outlook provides an interface for working with disk files that's similar to the Windows Explorer.

As you can see in **Figure 2.1**, the Outlook program window is divided into two main parts:

◆ The **Navigation pane** on the left, which displays icons for each Outlook folder and groups of shortcuts. A *shortcut* consists of an icon plus a text label. You can click an icon or shortcut link to quickly open a particular Outlook folder, file folder, or other item.

◆ The **folder view**, which displays the contents of the open folder. Sometimes the view is divided into smaller panes. For example, as shown in **Figure 2.2**, when the Inbox folder is open you can display a Reading pane at the right or bottom of the folder view, which lets you immediately read your messages without opening them.

Navigation pane      Folder pane      Reading pane

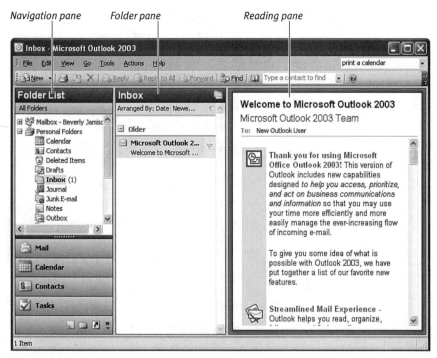

**Figure 2.2** The Inbox with the Reading Pane displayed at the right.

## ✔ Tips

- The Inbox, Drafts, Outbox, and Sent Items folders all store mail items, a category of Outlook items that includes email messages and faxes.

- Search folders help you organize messages. Search folders are really just a visual representation of a search, not a physical folder. Outlook includes a few predefined search folders, but you can create others using your own search conditions.

- Don't confuse an Outlook folder with a file folder. An Outlook folder stores Outlook items strictly within Outlook, whereas a file folder stores physical files on a local or network disk and can be accessed by any program. In this book, the term folder refers to an Outlook folder unless it's otherwise qualified.

- Later in the chapter, you'll learn how to open Outlook folders, and in the next two chapters, you'll learn how to work with Outlook items and the folders that contain them.

How Outlook Is Organized

# Learning Basic Windows and Office Techniques

Before you can learn the techniques specific to Outlook, you must be familiar with basic Windows and Office techniques. These are described in the following instructions.

### ✔ Tips

- Often, you can perform an Outlook operation using the mouse, a menu command, a toolbar button, or a keyboard command. I generally describe all the different methods so that you can choose your favorite.

- Methods using menu commands or toolbar buttons are the easiest to remember, because the menus and buttons provide visual cues. You do not need to memorize keyboard commands, but they are generally faster than using the toolbar. So, as you work with Outlook, you might want to gradually learn the keyboard commands to speed up your work.

## Using the Mouse

These are the terms for basic mouse operations that are used in this book:

- To *point to an object* on the screen means to move the tip of the mouse pointer over the object (**Figure 2.3**).

- To *click* means to press and release the left mouse button.

- To *double-click* means to press and release the left mouse button twice in rapid succession.

- To *click on an object* (or just *click an object*) means to point to the object and then click (**Figure 2.4**).

**Figure 2.3** Pointing to a menu command.

**Figure 2.4** Clicking a toolbar button.

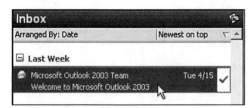

**Figure 2.5** Double-clicking a message in the inbox.

**Figure 2.6** Right-clicking a blank area to open a pop-up menu.

**Figure 2.7** The mouse pointer as it appears when you drag an Outlook item from one folder to another.

◆ To *double-click on an object* (or just *double-click an object*) means to point to the object and then double-click (**Figure 2.5**).

◆ To *right-click* means to click using the right mouse button (**Figure 2.6**).

◆ To *drag* means to point to an object or location, press the left mouse button, and then move the pointer while holding down the button (**Figure 2.7**).

◆ To *drop* means to release the mouse button after dragging to a destination location.

## ✔ Tip

■ The mouse pointer changes shape according to the part of the screen you point to, to indicate the particular action the mouse will perform. For instance, while over a toolbar button or menu, the pointer is usually a left-pointing arrow, while over text it's usually an I-beam, and while over a hyperlink it's usually a hand with an extended index finger. (A *hyperlink* is an object you click to open a specific document, page, or Web page.)

## To choose a menu command:

◆ Click the menu's label on the menu bar to open the menu, and then click the command. If the command is on a submenu, first point to the submenu label (marked with a triangle) to open the submenu, and then click the command (**Figure 2.8**).

## ✔ Tips

■ In this book, the phrase "Choose Tools > Organize" tells you to choose the Organize command on the Tools menu. And "Choose Actions > Junk E-mail > Add Sender to Blocked Senders List" tells you to choose the command shown in **Figure 2.8**.

■ A menu command followed by an ellipsis opens a dialog box to obtain additional information, rather than immediately carrying out an action.

■ If a menu command is unavailable, the label is displayed in light gray letters and you can't choose it.

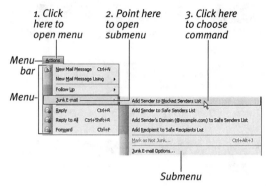

**Figure 2.8** Choosing a menu command on a submenu.

*To display all menu commands, double-click here...*

*or click here*

**Figure 2.9** Displaying all commands on a menu.

## To show all commands on a menu:

◆ To see all commands on a particular menu, open the menu by double-clicking the menu's label. By default, Outlook shows only the menu commands you use most frequently.

*or*

Click the bottom of the menu (marked with double down-arrows) (**Figure 2.9**).

*or*

Pause a few seconds after opening the menu. All the commands will then appear.

## ✔ Tips

■ If you want Outlook to always show all commands on a menu, choose Tools > Customize, and in the Options tab of the Customize dialog box, check the Always Show Full Menus option. (Dialog boxes are discussed later in this chapter.)

■ In the "Customizing the Toolbars and Menus" section of Chapter 14, "Customizing Outlook," you'll learn how to customize the Outlook menus to suit your work habits. I recommend waiting to do customizing until you finish working through this book, however, so that your menus will match the instructions you see in the book.

### To use a pop-up menu:

1. Right-click an object in the Outlook window.

   Outlook will display a pop-up menu of commands that are useful for working on whatever object underlies the mouse pointer. For example, if you right-click a message in your Inbox, Outlook will show a pop-up menu of commands for working with a message (**Figure 2.10**).

2. Choose (that is, click) the command you want to carry out.

### ✔ Tip

- A pop-up menu is also known as a *shortcut menu* or a *context menu* because the commands it shows depend upon the context of the object that you right-click.

## Using Toolbars

Outlook has three toolbars you can display:

- The **Standard toolbar** contains buttons for the most commonly used commands (**Figure 2.11**).

- The **Advanced toolbar** has buttons for less frequently used commands (**Figure 2.12**).

- The **Web toolbar** provides buttons for navigating through documents or Web pages (**Figure 2.13**). It's described in Chapter 13, "Exploring the Web in Outlook."

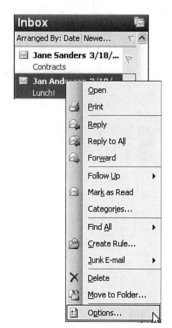

**Figure 2.10** The pop-up menu displayed when you right-click a message in the Inbox.

**Figure 2.11** The Standard toolbar.

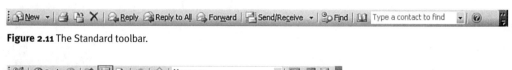

**Figure 2.12** The Advanced toolbar.

**Figure 2.13** The Web toolbar.

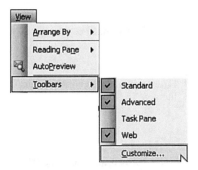

**Figure 2.14** Using the Toolbars submenu to display a toolbar.

**Figure 2.15** Using the pop-up menu to display a toolbar.

**Figure 2.16** Check marks indicating that the Standard and Advanced toolbars are displayed.

## ✔ Tips

■ The buttons displayed on the Standard and Advanced toolbars change according to the folder that's currently open. The toolbars provide the commands that are most useful for working with each type of information.

■ Outlook treats the Task pane as a toolbar, including it in the Toolbars menu. The Task pane offers Help, Research, and Search Results.

## To display a toolbar:

◆ If a toolbar you want to use isn't visible, choose View > Toolbars to open the Toolbars submenu, and then choose the name of the toolbar (**Figure 2.14**).

*or*

Right-click the toolbar area of the Outlook window and choose the name of the toolbar on the pop-up menu (**Figure 2.15**).

A check mark will appear next to the toolbar name on the menu to indicate that the toolbar is displayed (**Figure 2.16**).

## ✔ Tip

■ To hide a toolbar, choose the toolbar name from either the Toolbars submenu or the pop-up menu. The toolbar will be hidden, and the check mark will be removed.

### To execute a toolbar command:

◆ Click the Toolbar button (**Figure 2.17**).

### ✔ Tips

■ If the buttons belonging to a toolbar don't all fit within the area allotted to the toolbar in the program window, Outlook will display only the ones you've used most frequently. You can display the hidden buttons by clicking the right end of the toolbar (**Figure 2.18**). If you maximize Outlook, it will increase the available area on the toolbar, thereby allowing the toolbar to display more buttons.

■ To see the purpose of a toolbar button, point to it for a few seconds, and Outlook will display a ScreenTip describing the button (**Figure 2.19**), provided that the Show ScreenTips on Toolbars option is checked. (Access this option by choosing Tools > Customize and opening the Options tab in the Customize dialog box.)

■ Some toolbar buttons display a menu of commands or a list of items, rather than immediately carrying out an action. To display the menu or list, click the down-arrow to the right of the button (**Figure 2.20**). Then click the desired command or item.

■ Buttons that turn an option on or off appear normal when the option is off and have a box and colored highlight around them when the option is on. For example, when the Reading pane isn't displayed, the Reading Pane button appears normal. After you click this button to display the Reading pane, the button is highlighted and boxed.

**Figure 2.17** Clicking a toolbar button.

**Figure 2.18** Displaying hidden toolbar buttons.

**Figure 2.19** Displaying a ScreenTip.

**Figure 2.20** A toolbar button that displays a menu of commands.

■ If a button command isn't available, the button will be displayed in light gray, and clicking it will have no effect. For example, the Undo button on the Advanced toolbar will be displayed in light gray when there is no action to undo.

■ In Chapter 14 (the section "Customizing the Toolbars and Menus"), you'll learn how to move and customize the Outlook toolbars to suit your work habits. I recommend waiting to do this until you finish working through this book, however, so that the instructions you see in the book will match your toolbars.

**Figure 2.21** Executing a menu command using the keyboard.

## Using Keyboard Commands

Many keyboard commands consist of a single key. For example, you can view help by pressing the F1 key or close a dialog box by pressing the Esc key.

Other keyboard commands consist of two or three keys that you must press simultaneously. For example, you can copy text by pressing Ctr+C (that is, by pressing Ctrl and C simultaneously). And you can open the Address Book by pressing Ctrl+Shift+B (that is, by pressing Ctrl and Shift and B simultaneously).

### ✔ Tips

- You can execute any menu command by pressing Alt plus the underlined letters on the menu. For example, you can invoke the Edit > Copy menu command by first pressing Alt+E to open the Edit menu (E is underlined in the label for the Edit menu), and then pressing C (C is underlined in the Copy command label) (**Figure 2.21**).

- Many (but not all) of the Outlook menu commands display equivalent keyboard commands. For example, next to the Copy command on the Edit menu, Outlook displays an equivalent keyboard command, Ctrl+C (**Figure 2.21**).

- To obtain a concise list of Outlook keyboard commands, type the phrase "keyboard shortcuts" into the Type a Question for Help text box (right edge of the menu bar) and then choose the topic "Keyboard Shortcuts" from the Search Results pane. To create a printed copy, you can print out each of the subtopics.

# Working with Dialog Boxes

A dialog box is a window that Outlook temporarily opens on top of its main window to display information or to obtain information from you (**Figure 2.22** and **Figure 2.23**). You enter information into a dialog box by using the different types of controls it displays:

◆ You click a **command button** to carry out an action, such as closing the dialog box and applying its settings (the OK button), closing the dialog box and discarding its settings (the Cancel button), or opening another dialog box (**Figure 2.22**).

◆ You check or uncheck a **check box** to turn an independent option on or off (**Figure 2.22**). To check or uncheck a check box, simply click on any part of the label or the check box itself.

◆ You select an **option button** (also quaintly known as a **radio button**) to choose one of a group of mutually exclusive options (**Figure 2.23**). To select an option button, click on any part of the label or the button itself. A dot will appear in the button, and the dot from the previously selected option button will be removed.

◆ You click and type into a **text box** to supply textual information (**Figure 2.22**).

◆ Sometimes, a pair of **spin buttons** are displayed to the right of a text box to help you enter a numeric value (**Figure 2.24**).

◆ You click an item displayed in a list to select it (**Figure 2.23**). Selecting a **list item** highlights it. Sometimes double-clicking a list item will select the item, close the dialog box, and apply the settings.

*Check boxes*     *Drop-down list*

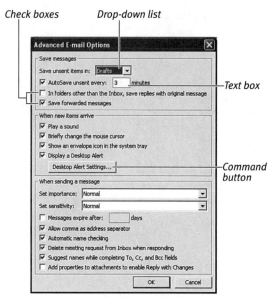

*Text box*

*Command button*

**Figure 2.22** Dialog box controls.

*Option buttons*

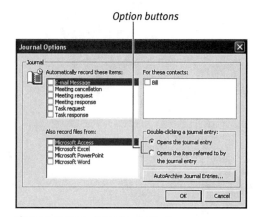

**Figure 2.23** More dialog box controls.

*Combination of text box and Spin buttons*

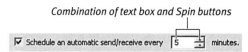

**Figure 2.24** Even more dialog box controls.

Tabs      Help    Close

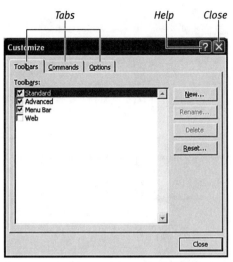

**Figure 2.25** Opening a tab in a tabbed dialog box.

◆ You open a list box and then click an item in the list to select it (**Figure 2.22**). To open a list box (that is, to drop it down and display the list items), click the down-arrow at the right end.

◆ Some dialog boxes contain several tabs, each of which displays a separate set of controls. For example, the dialog box shown in **Figure 2.25** has three tabs. To open a tab and display the controls it contains, click the label at the top of the tab.

### ✔ Tips

■ With most dialog boxes, you must click the OK, Close, or Cancel button to remove the dialog box before you can continue working in Outlook.

■ Generally, pressing Enter while a dialog box is displayed is equivalent to clicking the OK button (the dialog box is closed and its settings are applied). Pressing Esc or clicking the Close button is equivalent to clicking the Cancel button (the dialog box is closed and its settings are discarded).

■ Some dialog boxes have a Close, instead of an OK, button at the bottom (**Figure 2.25**). In this situation, pressing Enter while the dialog box is displayed is equivalent to clicking the Close button (the dialog box is closed and its settings are saved).

■ To get help while you're working with a dialog box, click the Help button near the upper-right corner of the dialog box and then click the control or area of the dialog box you want to learn about.

LEARNING BASIC OFFICE TECHNIQUES

# Using the Assistance Pane

Outlook includes an Assistance pane that offers access to the Help content, both online and offline, for Outlook. The Assistance pane (**Figure 2.26**) is actually one of three panes comprising the Task pane.

## ✔ Tips

- Open the Assistance pane by choosing Help > Microsoft Outlook Help or by pressing F1. The Assistance pane by default shows local Help content as well as links to information on the Office Online Web site.

- Choose between the Assistance pane and the other two panes in the Task pane by clicking the arrow button at the top of the pane and choosing the desired pane.

**Figure 2.26** The three Assistance panes comprising the Task pane.

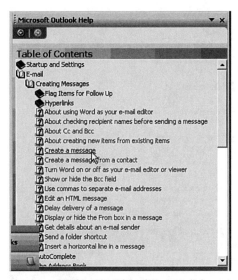

**Figure 2.27** Clicking the Table of Contents link.

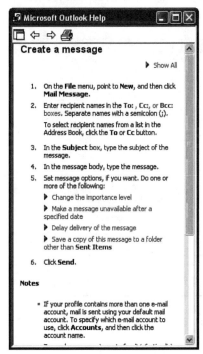

**Figure 2.28** The Help topic content displayed in its own window.

## To get help with Outlook:

1. Press F1 or choose Help > Microsoft Outlook Help.

2. Click the Table of Contents link to open the Help Table of Contents (**Figure 2.27**).

3. Select the topic for which you need help to expand it and view the Help content for the topic. The topic appears in its own window (**Figure 2.28**).

4. Click the Print button on the toolbar if you want to print the Help topic.

## ✔ Tips

■ Click on an expanded topic list to collapse the list.

■ Click the Back button just above the Table of Contents to return to the Assistance pane, where you can perform searches or view online Help links.

**USING THE ASSISTANCE PANE**

## To search for Help topics:

1. Open the Assistance pane by pressing F1 or choosing Help > Microsoft Outlook Help.

2. Type a search word or phrase in the Search text box, and click the Start Searching button (green and white arrow).

3. In the Search Results pane (**Figure 2.29**), click the link for the topic you want to view to open the topic in a separate window.

4. Click the Back button to enter another search word or phrase or use other links in the Assistance pane.

## ✔ Tip

■ Use the small up- and down-arrow buttons at the top and bottom of the Assistance pane to scroll through the pane and view other links and topics.

## To get information about your copy of Outlook:

1. Choose Help > About Microsoft Outlook to display the About Microsoft Office Outlook dialog box (**Figure 2.30**).

2. View the version of Outlook in the top line of the dialog box, and view the Product ID number in the box labeled "This product is licensed to." Microsoft Support Services require that you provide this number when calling for technical support.

3. Click Tech Support to open a Help topic page that lists technical support options, phone numbers, and other contact information for Outlook technical support.

**Figure 2.29** Clicking the link for the topic you want to view.

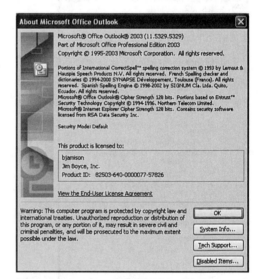

**Figure 2.30** The About Microsoft Office Outlook dialog box.

**Figure 2.31** The Office Assistant, at your service.

**Figure 2.32** The Office Assistant displaying a balloon for you to ask your question.

*Search topic*

**Figure 2.33** A list of topics matching the question that was typed.

# Consulting the Assistant

You can get help on almost any feature of Outlook by using the Office Assistant (**Figure 2.31**).

## ✔ Tips

■ If you want to start exploring Outlook on your own, before working though this book, I recommend that you read the instructions on using the Assistant and on opening folders—both given later in this chapter. You'll find most commands you need on the menus and on the Standard toolbar. Use the Assistant whenever you need help!

■ The Office Assistant is not installed by default in a Typical installation, but Setup will add the Assistant the first time you try to use it.

## To use the Assistant:

1. If the Assistant is visible, click on it.

   *or*

   If the Assistant is hidden, choose Help > Show the Office Assistant. The Assistant will display a help balloon (**Figure 2.32**).

2. Type a question into the text box in the Assistant's balloon, and click the Search button.

   You don't have to type a full sentence, but try to be specific so that the Assistant can find a shorter, more appropriate list of topics. For example, if you want to print your Calendar folder, type the phrase "print calendar folder" rather than just "print."

   The balloon will display a list of topics matching your question. **Figure 2.33** shows the topics displayed for "print calendar folder."

*continues on next page*

CONSULTING THE ASSISTANT

**3.** Click the most appropriate of the listed topics to view the help information. (If the topics don't all fit in the balloon, you can click See More to view additional topics.)

The help text will generally be displayed in the Microsoft Outlook Help window (**Figure 2.34**).

**4.** When you're done reading the help text, remove the Microsoft Outlook Help window by clicking the Close button in the upper-right corner of the window.

**Figure 2.34** The Microsoft Outlook Help window.

## ✔ Tips

■ Like a cat, the Assistant tends to perch right where you're working. To move it, drag the main Assistant body (not the balloon) to another part of the screen.

■ You can temporarily hide the Assistant by choosing Help > Hide The Office Assistant.

■ An Outlook form (described in Chapter 3, "Working with Outlook Items") also has a Help menu, which you can use instead of the Help menu in the main Outlook window.

■ The Assistant observes you working and occasionally offers a tip. When it has a tip to provide, a light bulb appears next to the Assistant (or next to the Microsoft Outlook Help button if the Assistant is hidden). Click the light bulb to see the tip.

■ To print a help topic, click the Print button at the top of the Microsoft Outlook Help window.

■ For information on choosing a different Assistant character, or on modifying the Assistant's behavior, see the section "Changing the Office Assistant" in Appendix A, "Configuring Outlook." (Be sure to check this section if the Assistant isn't working as described here.)

# Getting Around in Outlook

The first step in working with any kind of information in Outlook is to open the appropriate folder. For example, if you want to read or send email messages, open the Inbox folder. If you want to see your appointments for the day, open the Calendar folder. If you want to find out what you need to get done this week, open the Tasks folder.

The following instructions show you the different ways to open an Outlook folder. These techniques will let you move around in Outlook and explore the different types of information it manages.

### ✔ Tips

■ In Chapter 3 you'll learn how to work with Outlook items, and in Chapter 4, "Working with Outlook Folders," you'll learn how to modify the Outlook folders that contain items.

## Opening an Outlook folder

The Outlook shortcuts are divided into several groups. By default, shortcuts to the Outlook folders are located within:

◆ The **Navigation pane,** which contains buttons for the general-purpose Outlook folders: Inbox (Mail), Calendar, Contacts, Tasks, Notes, Folder List, and Journal.

◆ The **Shortcuts pane,** which contains shortcuts to additional items, including Outlook Today and the Outlook Update page on Microsoft's Web site.

### To open an Outlook folder:

1. In the Navigation pane, drag the top of the folder button area up, if needed, to locate the button for the folder you want to open (**Figure 2.35**).

2. Click the button for the folder you want to open.

   Outlook will then display the contents of that folder on the right. (For example, in **Figure 2.2**, the Inbox folder is opened, and the messages it contains are displayed.)

### ✔ Tips

- You can hide or display the Navigation pane by choosing View > Navigation pane.

- Your groups and shortcuts might be different from those described here. For example, you might have added additional shortcuts for file folders or other Outlook folders to the Shortcuts list.

- Outlook Bar shortcuts can directly open disk files or Web pages, as well as folders. An example is the Outlook Update shortcut in the default My Shortcuts group, which opens the Outlook Update Web site when you click it.

- You can open an Outlook folder in a separate Outlook window by right-clicking the folder's shortcut in the Navigation pane and then choosing Open In New Window from the pop-up menu. This technique allows you to work with a second folder without disturbing your view of the currently opened folder.

- In Chapter 14 (the section "Modifying the Navigation Pane") you'll learn how to add, remove, and modify groups and shortcuts in the Navigation pane. I recommend waiting to do this until you finish working through this book, however, so that your Navigation pane will match the default one described in here (unless, of course, your Navigation pane is already different).

**Figure 2.35** Drag the top of the folder button up to display more folders.

## Other Ways to Open Folders

Outlook provides several additional ways to open an Outlook folder.

◆ You can select a folder in the **Folder List**, which displays a hierarchical list of folders. When displayed, the Folder List appears in the top area of the Navigation pane. The Folder List lets you access any Outlook folder, not just those for which icons are included in the Navigation pane.

  Outlook folders are organized in a hierarchy. That is, folders can contain other folders, as well as Outlook items. A single root folder resides at the top of the hierarchy (Personal Folders if you use a PST or Mailbox if you use Exchange Server to store your Outlook data), which contains everything.

◆ You can use the **Go To Folder** dialog box to locate and open a specific folder. This method is useful for opening a folder that doesn't have an icon on the Navigation pane.

◆ You can **navigate** through folders that you've previously opened, using buttons on the Advanced toolbar or commands on the Go To submenu of the View menu.

◆ You can open the next folder up in the hierarchy of your Outlook or file folders by clicking the **Up One Level button**.

### ✔ Tips

■ From anywhere in Outlook, you can open the Outlook Today folder by clicking the Outlook Today button on the Advanced toolbar, and you can open the Inbox folder by pressing Ctrl+Shift+I.

■ You can open the Inbox, Calendar, Contacts, Notes, Tasks, or Journal folder by opening the Go menu and choosing the folder name from the submenu.

**GETTING AROUND IN OUTLOOK**

## To open a folder using the Folder List:

1. Display the Folder List by clicking the Folder List button on the Navigation pane (**Figure 2.36**).

   *or*

   Display the Folder List by clicking the Folder List button on the Advanced toolbar or by choosing Go > Folder List.

   Outlook does not display a particular folder until you click it in the Folder List (**Figure 2.37**).

2. To expand or collapse a branch of the folder hierarchy in the Folder List, click the + or – symbol next to the folder's name (**Figure 2.38**).

3. To open a folder, click on it in the Folder List.

   Outlook then displays the contents of that folder.

## ✔ Tips

- Drag the top of the button bar down in the Navigation pane to make more room for the Folder List. Or, click Configure Buttons at the bottom of the Navigation pane and choose Show Fewer Buttons to resize the button area and make more room for the Folder List.

- The bottom of the Folder List contains links that enable you to manage data files (such as add another PST) and view the amount of space used by each folder.

**Figure 2.36** Click the Folder List button to open the Folder List.

**Figure 2.37** Display a folder by clicking It in the Folder List.

**Figure 2.38** Expanding and collapsing branches of the folder hierarchy in the Folder List.

**Figure 2.39** Displaying a folder's name in bold and indicating the number of unread messages it contains.

**Figure 2.40** The Go To Folder dialog box.

■ If you use Exchange Server, you can access public folders on the Exchange Server by clicking on the folder in the Folder List. The Public Folders branch appears at the bottom of the Folder List.

■ If an Outlook folder contains one or more unread messages, the Folder List displays the folder's name in bold and indicates the number of unread messages it contains. An example is the Deleted Items folder shown in **Figure 2.39**. (Exception: The Outbox or Drafts folder is displayed in bold if it contains any messages, and the number shown is the total number of messages it contains.)

## To locate and open a specific folder using the Go To Folder dialog box:

1. Choose Go > Folder or press Ctrl+Y to open the Go To Folder dialog box (**Figure 2.40**).

2. In the list of folders, click the one you want to open. Use the + and – signs in the list to expand and collapse the list as needed.

   or

   Select the name of the folder from the drop-down list of the Folder Name list box. This list contains the names of folders you've recently opened.

   or

   Select the name of the folder in the hierarchical list displayed below the Folder Name list box.

3. Click the OK button.

## To navigate through previously opened folders:

1. To reopen the folder you last had open, click the Back button on the Advanced toolbar (**Figure 2.41**).

2. After you've clicked the Back button one or more times to go back through previously opened folders, you can go forward again by clicking the Forward button on the Advanced toolbar.

## To open the next folder up in the folder hierarchy:

◆ Click the Up One Level button on the Advanced toolbar.

For example, if the Inbox is open, clicking this button will open Outlook Today, because Inbox is contained within Outlook Today in the hierarchy of Outlook folders (see the Folder List in **Figure 2.36**). Similarly, if a particular public folder is open, clicking this button will open All Public Folders, because All Public Folders is the root of the public folder hierarchy.

## ✔ Tip

■ You can easily move items from one folder to another with the Folder List. Display the folder list, open the folder where the item is located, and then drag it to the destination folder in the Folder List.

*Back*  *Up One Level*

**Figure 2.41** Click the Back button to reopen the folder you last had open.

# WORKING WITH OUTLOOK ITEMS

# 3

Outlook items are the individual pieces of information stored in your Outlook folders—for example, email messages in your Inbox folder, appointments in your Calendar folder, and task descriptions in your Tasks folder.

The first step in working with a particular type of Outlook item is to open the appropriate folder. Chapter 2, "Getting Started Using Outlook," (in the section "How to Get Around in Outlook") described the different ways to locate and open folders. Specifically, you should open the:

- ◆ **Inbox**, **Drafts**, **Outbox**, or **Sent Items** folder to work with email

- ◆ **Calendar** folder to work with appointments, events, or meetings

- ◆ **Contacts** folder to work with contact descriptions (each of which stores information on a person or company) or distribution lists (each of which stores an entire set of addresses)

- ◆ **Tasks** folder to work with task descriptions

- ◆ **Journal** folder to work with journal entries

- ◆ **Notes** folder to work with text notes

- ◆ **Deleted Items** folder to work with items you've removed from other folders

In this chapter you'll learn how to:

◆ Create new Outlook items

◆ Open items in an Outlook form

◆ Edit items

◆ Copy or move items

◆ Remove items, temporarily or permanently

◆ Archive items, automatically or manually

◆ Alter the overall organization of items by switching views

◆ Modify the way items are displayed in a particular view by sorting, filtering, or grouping them

◆ Work with items using the Organize Page

◆ Find Outlook items as well as disk files

## ✔ Tips

■ This is the first of two chapters that cover the general Outlook techniques you use when working with almost any type of information. In this chapter, you learn how to work with the items in Outlook folders. In Chapter 4, "Working with Outlook Folders," you learn how to work with the folders themselves.

■ I recommend quickly reading through Chapters 3 and 4 now and referring back to them frequently once you start working with the specific types of Outlook information in Chapters 5 through 11.

■ The folders listed on the previous page refer only to the default folders created by Outlook. In Chapter 4, you'll learn how to create new folders to store specific types of Outlook information.

■ The Outlook Today folder is a special case. Rather than storing a particular type of Outlook item, it displays a page that gives you access to the current information in several commonly used folders.

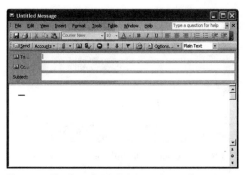

**Figure 3.1** The form for defining a new email message.

**Figure 3.2** The form for defining a new appointment.

**Figure 3.3** The form for defining a new note.

# Creating Items

You enter information into Outlook by creating new Outlook *items*. You typically define the information for a new item in a separate window known as a *form*. A form displays a set of controls (text boxes, list boxes, option buttons, and so on) in which you enter the item information. Each piece of information that you enter through a control—such as the subject of an email message, the start time of an appointment, or the priority of a task—is known as a *field*. A form also provides menu commands and toolbar buttons to assist you in adding, editing, and formatting the information and in working with the item in various ways.

Each type of item—for example, an email message, an appointment, or a note—has a different form, one that's designed specifically for entering, editing, and viewing the item's information (**Figures 3.1 through 3.3**).

## ✔ Tips

- For a description of the different controls you use for entering information, see the section "Working with Dialog Boxes" in Chapter 2.

- In a form, if a toolbar you want to use isn't visible, choose View > Toolbars on the form's menu, and then choose the name of the toolbar from the submenu. Or, right-click the toolbar area of the form, and choose the name of the toolbar from the pop-up menu.

- In addition to menu commands for working directly with the opened item, most forms also provide general-purpose commands that are the same as menu commands found on the main Outlook window.

*continues on next page*

CREATING ITEMS

These commands include

▲ The commands on the File > New submenu for creating new Outlook items

▲ Tools > Address Book for opening the Address Book dialog box

▲ Tools > Customize for customizing the Outlook toolbars and menus

▲ The commands on the Help menu for obtaining online help

## To create an item:

1. Open the folder in which you want to create the new item.

   (To create a new email or fax message, you can open any mail-item folder—Inbox, Drafts, Outbox, or Sent Items.)

2. To create the default type of item for the opened folder, click the New button on the Standard toolbar or press Ctrl+N.

   The following are the default item types for the Outlook folders:

   ▲ Inbox, Drafts, Outbox, or Sent Items: email message

   ▲ Calendar: appointment

   ▲ Contacts: contact

   ▲ Tasks: task

   ▲ Journal: journal entry

   ▲ Notes: note

   *or*

   If the folder manages several types of items, to create a specific type of item, choose the appropriate command from the Actions menu. For example, if you've opened a mail-item folder, such as Inbox, you can choose Actions > Forward to send your mail message to another email account (**Figure 3.4**). Or, if you've opened the Calendar folder, you can choose Actions > New All Day Event to create an event (**Figure 3.5**).

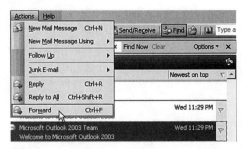

**Figure 3.4** The Actions menu when the Inbox folder is opened.

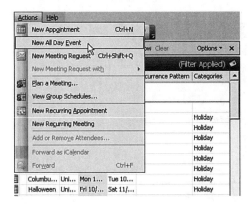

**Figure 3.5** The Actions menu when the Calendar folder is opened.

**Figure 3.6** The Actions menu when the Contacts folder is opened.

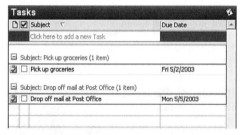

**Figure 3.7** You can create a new task by clicking the top row of the information viewer and entering information.

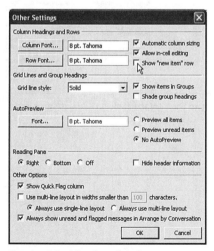

**Figure 3.8** Enabling "new item" row.

*or*

If you've opened the Contacts folder, you can choose Actions > New Distribution List to create a distribution list (**Figure 3.6**). (An Outlook form also has an Actions menu you can use.)

Outlook will then open an empty form of the appropriate type for you to fill in (**Figures 3.1–3.3**).

**3.** Enter the item's information and close the form.

For instructions on entering the item's information, see "Editing Items," later in the chapter. You typically close the form by clicking the Save and Close button, but see "Editing Items" for exceptions.

Once you've created a new item and closed the form, the item is displayed— along with the other items in the opened folder—in the Information Viewer of the Outlook window. In "Opening Items," later in the chapter, you'll learn how to reopen an item in a form so you can view or edit any of its information.

## ✔ Tips

■ In a table view (a view with rows and columns such as the Phone List view shown in **Figure 3.46**, later in the chapter) you can create a new item and enter the basic item information right in the Information Viewer, without opening a form. To do this, you click the top table row (usually labeled Click Here to Add a New Item), enter information into the fields shown, and press Enter (**Figure 3.7**). The Show "new item" Row option, however, must be enabled for the current view (**Figure 3.8**). You access this option by choosing View > Arrange By > Current View > Customize Current View and clicking the Other Settings button.

*continues on next page*

**CREATING ITEMS**

- You can create almost any type of item, regardless of which folder is currently open, by clicking the down-arrow next to the New button on the Standard toolbar, and then choosing the item type from the drop-down menu (**Figure 3.9**). Alternatively, you can use the identical New submenu on the File menu in the Outlook window or in an Outlook form.

- You can create many different types of Outlook items, also regardless of which folder is open, by using the keyboard commands listed on the menu shown in **Figure 3.9**. Note, however, that if a mail-item folder isn't currently open, you'll need to press Ctrl+Shift+M to create a new email message (rather than Ctrl+N).

- You can quickly create a new item based on an existing item of a different type by dragging the existing item from the opened folder and dropping it on the Outlook Bar shortcut for a folder of a different type. For example, if you open the Inbox, drag an email message from the Inbox, and drop it on the Contacts shortcut, Outlook creates a new contact that already contains the name and email address of the person who sent you the message. Similarly, if you drag an appointment from the Calendar folder and drop it on the Tasks shortcut, Outlook creates a new task that contains the description and date from the appointment (the appointment date becomes the due date of the task).

- You can get a head start in creating a new item by making a copy of an existing item in the same type of folder. For instance, to create a new contact that has the same address, telephone, and web site as an existing contact, you could make a copy of the existing contact and then quickly edit the copy. See "Copying and Moving Items," later in the chapter.

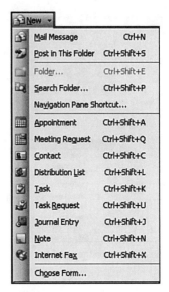

**Figure 3.9** The menu that drops down from the New button. This is how the menu appears when a mail-item folder such as Inbox is open.

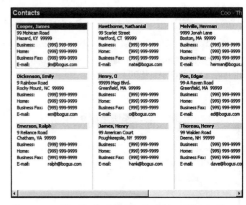

**Figure 3.10** The Contacts folder in Address Cards view.

CREATING ITEMS

**Figure 3.11** The Contact form, however, shows and lets you edit all contact information.

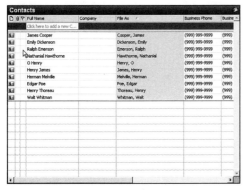

**Figure 3.12** Double-click a contact item dis-played in the Information Viewer to open it.

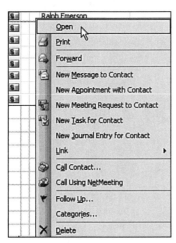

**Figure 3.13** Open a Contact item by choosing Open from the pop-up menu.

# Opening Items

When you open a folder, the Outlook Information Viewer displays the items it contains in a table, timeline, or other arrangement. Typically it shows only a portion of each item's information and allows only minor editing, if any (**Figure 3.10**). To view all of an item's information or to fully edit the item, you need to open it. When you open an item, Outlook displays it in the appropriate form for the particular type of item (**Figure 3.11**).

### To open an item:

◆ Double-click on the item in the Information Viewer (**Figure 3.12**).

 *or*

 Click the item to select it (that is, highlight it), and press Enter or Ctrl+O.

 *or*

 Right-click the item, and choose Open from the pop-up menu (**Figure 3.13**).

 Once the item is opened in the form, you can view it or edit it as described in "Editing Items," later in the chapter.

### ✔ Tips

■ You can open several items at once by selecting all of them before pressing Enter or Ctrl+O, or before right-clicking them and choosing Open from the pop-up menu. You can close all open items by choosing File > Close All Items.

■ To select several adjoining items displayed in the Information Viewer, click the first one to select it and then expand the selection by pressing the appropriate arrow key while holding down Shift. Or, click the first item in the group and, while holding down the Shift key, click the last item.

*continues on next page*

- To select several non-adjoining items, click the first one to select it and then, while holding down the Ctrl key, click each additional item.

- To select all items in the open folder, choose Edit > Select All or press Ctrl+A.

- If you've opened an existing item in a form, you can view other items in the same folder within that form. To view the previous or next item in the folder, click the Previous Item button or the Next Item button on the form's Standard toolbar. To view a specific type of item, click the down arrow next to the Previous Item or Next Item button and choose a command from the drop-down menu (**Figure 3.14**). The commands on the drop-down menus are also found on the Previous and Next submenus of the form's View menu.

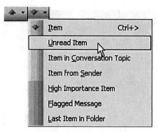

**Figure 3.14** Opening the next unread item in the Inbox folder. (In this example, the form is displaying a message in the Inbox folder.)

**Figure 3.15** Saving your changes and closing an Appointment form.

# Editing Items

The following instructions show you how to edit a new item that you've just created in an empty form or an existing item that you've opened in a form.

### ✔ Tip

- You can edit fields displayed in the Information Viewer, without opening the item in a form, by clicking on the field and typing or selecting a new value. In the Calendar folder, for example, you can click on the subject field of an appointment and edit the text. To do this in most views, however, the Allow In-Cell Editing option must be checked. You access this option by choosing View > Arrange By > Current View > Customize Current View and clicking the Other Settings button.

### To edit a new or existing item:

1. Open the item in a form. To open a new item in an empty form, follow the instructions given in "Creating Items." To open an existing item, follow the instructions given in "Opening Items."

2. Add, modify, or remove information within the controls displayed in the form.

   Upcoming sections in this chapter explain the general techniques that you can use in almost any form. Chapters 3 through 11 describe in detail the forms for each type of Outlook item and explain the techniques unique to particular types of items.

3. Save your changes and close the form. You typically do this by clicking the Save and Close button on the form's Standard toolbar (**Figure 3.15**).

*continues on next page*

EDITING ITEMS

**4.** Some forms, however, have different procedures. For example, in the Message form you generally click the Send button on the Standard toolbar to save and send the message, as well as to close the form (**Figure 3.16**). And in a Notes form, you click the Close button in the upper-right corner of the form to save the note and close the form (**Figure 3.17**).

## ✔ Tips

■ You can save your work without closing the form by choosing File > Save. Or, you can close the form and discard any unsaved changes by clicking the Close button in the upper-right corner of the form, or by choosing File > Close, or by pressing Esc or Alt+F4. Outlook will ask whether you want to save your changes. (These instructions don't apply to a Notes form.)

■ You can undo your most recent editing action in a form by choosing Edit > Undo or pressing Ctrl+Z. And you can reverse the effect of the Undo command by immediately choosing Edit > Redo or pressing Ctrl+Y. (In a Notes form, only the keyboard commands are available.)

■ To enter a date or time into a date or time field (for example, the due date or starting time of an appointment), you can type a normal expression such as "two weeks from now" or "noon" and Outlook will convert it to the actual date or time.

■ In the large text box in a form (for example, the text box where you enter the body of your message in a Message form) or in a note, you can enter a link to a Web page or an email address. To do this, just type the full Internet address (for example, http:// ourworld.compuserve.com/homepages/ mjy/ or mailto:mjy@compuserve.com) and Outlook will convert it to an underlined hyperlink that you can click to open the Web page in your browser or to send an email message to the address (**Figure 3.18**).

**Figure 3.16** Saving and sending a message, and closing the Message form.

**Figure 3.17** Saving your changes and closing a Notes form.

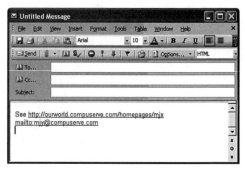

**Figure 3.18** Typing a hyperlink into the large text box of an appointment.

*Insertion point*

Company:    Acme Axe Handles|

**Figure 3.19** The insertion point that appears when you click a text box.

■ In the large text box in a form, you can search for specific text by choosing Edit > Find on the form's menu or by pressing F4. To find additional occurrences of the same text, choose Edit > Find Next or press Shift+F4.

### To enter or edit text in a text box:

**1.** Click on the text box to activate it.

The *insertion point*—a blinking vertical line—will appear in the box (**Figure 3.19**).

**2.** If you want to insert or delete text at a particular position within existing text, move the insertion point to that position by clicking on the position or by pressing the appropriate arrow key.

**3.** Type the text you want to enter.

Each character will be inserted at the position of the insertion point.

**4.** To erase text, press Backspace to delete the character preceding the insertion point, or press Delete to delete the character following the insertion point.

### ✔ Tip

■ These instructions also apply to entering text into a Notes form, which consists of a single text box.

**EDITING ITEMS**

# Selecting Text

To perform an operation on a block of text in a text box—for example, formatting it, copying it, deleting it, or checking its spelling—you must first select (that is, highlight) the text (**Figure 3.20**).

## To select text:

◆ Place the insertion point at the beginning or end of the text, and extend the highlight over the text by pressing the appropriate arrow key while holding down Shift.

*or*

Use the mouse to drag the highlight over the text.

## ✔ Tips

■ You can quickly select a single word by double-clicking it.

■ You can select all text in the active text box by choosing Edit > Select All or pressing Ctrl+A. (In a Notes form, only the keyboard command is available.)

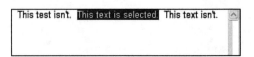

**Figure 3.20** Selected text in a text box.

# Formatting Text

You can format—modify the appearance of—the text you type into the large text box in an Outlook form. You can format individual characters or paragraphs (**Figure 3.21**).

### ✔ Tips

- You can't format the text for a Notes item. You can change only the background color of the note.

- The available formatting commands for a message depend on the editor and email format you're using, as explained in the section "Modifying the Format and Editor for Email Messages" in Chapter 6, "Using the Inbox to Manage Messages."

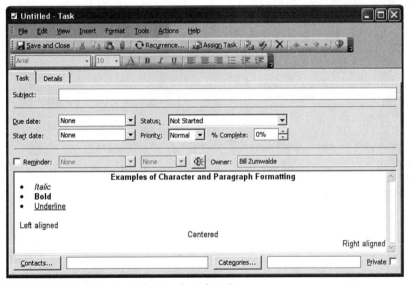

**Figure 3.21** Formatted text in the large text box of a task.

## To format text in a form's large text box:

1. Select existing text to format.

   *or*

   Place the insertion point at the position where you want to type new text.

2. To format the individual characters, choose Format > Font to open the Font dialog box (**Figure 3.22**). Select character formatting options using the list boxes and check boxes until the text in the Sample area of the dialog box has the look you want, and then click the OK button.

3. To change the paragraph alignment or to create a bulleted list, choose Font > Paragraph, select the desired options in the Paragraph dialog box (**Figure 3.23**), and then click the OK button.

   Outlook will then apply the new formatting to the selection (if you selected text) or to the characters you subsequently type at the current position of the insertion point.

### ✔ Tip

■ Rather than using a dialog box in steps 2 and 3, you can format by clicking buttons on the Formatting toolbar (**Figure 3.24**). Choose View > Toolbars > Formatting to display the Formatting toolbar.

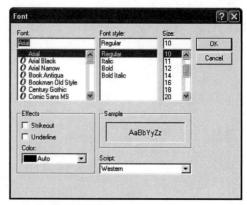

**Figure 3.22** The Font dialog box.

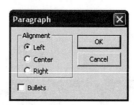

**Figure 3.23** The Paragraph dialog box.

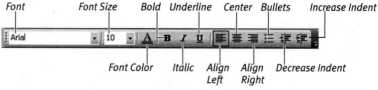

**Figure 3.24** The Formatting toolbar displayed in a form.

FORMATTING TEXT

*Paste all stored blocks*

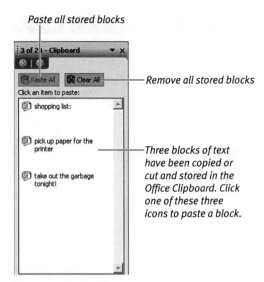

*Remove all stored blocks*

*Three blocks of text have been copied or cut and stored in the Office Clipboard. Click one of these three icons to paste a block.*

**Figure 3.25** Use the Clipboard task pane to paste a previously copied or cut block of text. If you place the mouse pointer over the icon for a particular block of text, the text will be shown in a ScreenTip.

# Copying and Moving Text

After you've typed information into a text box in an Outlook form, you can copy or move the text to another location within the same text box, within another text box, or even within a different Windows program.

### To copy or move text:

1. In a text box, select the text that you want to copy or move.

2. To copy the text, choose Edit > Copy or press Ctrl+C.

   *or*

   To move the text, choose Edit > Cut or press Ctrl+X.

3. Place the insertion point where you want to insert the copied or moved text.

   This can be within any text box, not just the one in which you copied or cut the text. The easiest way is to just click on the target position.

4. Choose Edit > Paste, or press Ctrl+V.

### ✔ Tips

- Outlook stores your 24 most recently copied or cut blocks of text. If you have copied or cut several blocks of text, you can use the Clipboard task pane to paste any of these blocks or all of them (**Figure 3.25**). (Pasting using Edit > Paste or Ctrl+V pastes only the most recently copied or cut block.)

- You can copy or move text or graphics between separate Windows programs. For example, you could copy a block of graphics from a paint program and then paste it into the large text box in an Outlook form.

- To remove the selected block of text, choose Edit > Clear or press Delete.

**COPYING AND MOVING TEXT**

# Checking Spelling

Before you send an email message or save an Outlook item such as an appointment or contact, you'd be wise to check your spelling.

### To check your spelling:

1. To check the spelling of the text in all text boxes within a form, place the insertion point within any text box.

   *or*

   To check the spelling of a specific block of text within a text box, select that text.

2. Choose Tools > Spelling, or press F7.

   The spelling checker will then check the spelling of each word. For each word that the spelling checker can't find in its dictionary, it displays the Spelling dialog box (**Figure 3.26**).

3. Use the Spelling dialog box as follows:

   ▲ To correct the spelling, click a spelling in the Suggestions list or type a correct spelling into the Change To text box, and then click either Change to change the current occurrence of the word or Change All to change all occurrences.

   ▲ To leave the word unchanged, click Ignore if you want to skip the current occurrence of the word or click Ignore All if you want to skip all occurrences.

   ▲ To ignore the word and add it to the spelling checker's custom dictionary, so that it will no longer be flagged as a misspelling, click Add.

**Figure 3.26** The Spelling dialog box.

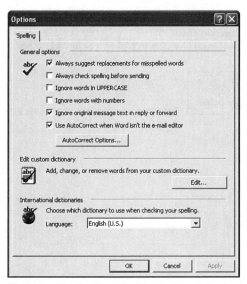

**Figure 3.27** The Spelling tab of the Options dialog box.

▲ To undo the previous spelling correction or return to the last word you reviewed, click Undo Last.

▲ To open the Spelling tab of the Options dialog box (**Figure 3.27**), where you can set spelling options, click Options.

▲ To cancel the spelling check, click Cancel.

## ✔ Tips

■ You can also set spelling options by choosing Tools > Options and opening the Spelling tab.

■ You can't check spelling in a Notes item.

# Inserting Files, Items, and Objects

You can insert any of the following into the large text box in an Outlook form:

◆ A **file from disk** as:

▲ *Text*: The full text from the file is inserted and displayed in the text box.

▲ *An attachment*: The text box stores a copy of the file, which it displays as an icon that you can double-click to open the copy (**Figure 3.28**).

▲ *A personal folder item shortcut*: The text box stores only the location of the original file, which it displays as a shortcut icon that you can double-click to open the original item (**Figure 3.29**). If you send the item to someone else, however, they will not have access to the referenced item.

◆ Another **Outlook item** as text, as an attachment, or as a shortcut. For example, you might insert an appointment into an email message sent to another Outlook user, so that the appointment can be added to his or her Calendar folder.

**Figure 3.28** An icon for an attached file.

**Figure 3.29** An icon for a shortcut to a file.

**Figure 3.30** An embedded object from the Clip Gallery inserted into a text box in a form.

◆ A **linked or embedded object**.

   ▲ A *linked object* displays data that is stored in a separate source document. If you modify the data in the source document, the linked object in the item is updated to match the source document. For example, you can insert a linked object that displays as an Excel workbook. Essentially, the link is really just a shortcut.

   ▲ An *embedded object* is data that is stored and displayed within the Outlook item but is created and edited in a separate source program. For example, you could embed a bitmap Image that is created and modified by the Paint program (**Figure 3.30**), or embed a document created in Word. Essentially, an embedded object is a copy of the object that is inserted into the Outlook item.

## ✔ Tip

■ If you're creating an email message in the Message form, avoid inserting a shortcut or a linked or embedded object, because the message recipient might not have access to the data or program required to view or edit the information.

## To insert a file:

1. Place the insertion point at the position where you want to insert the file in the large text box.

2. Choose Insert > Insert File, or click the Insert File button on the Standard toolbar.

3. In the Insert File dialog box (**Figure 3.31**), select the file you want to insert.

4. Click the Insert button to insert the file as an attachment.

   *or*

   Click the down arrow on the Insert button and select the way you want to insert the file (**Figure 3.32**). Note that when inserting a file into a form, clicking the button or selecting Insert has the same effect as selecting Insert As Attachment.

## ✔ Tips

- You can also insert a file as an attachment by dragging the filename from a file folder displayed in Outlook, or from the Windows Explorer or a file folder, and dropping it in the large text box in the form.

- When you drag an object from one window to another, if the target window is hidden on the screen, drag the object to the window's button on the Windows Taskbar and hold it there, keeping the mouse button pressed. After a few seconds, the target window will be activated and you can complete the drag operation.

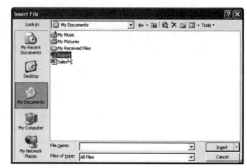

**Figure 3.31** The Insert File dialog box.

**Figure 3.32** Opening the drop-down menu to choose the method for inserting the file.

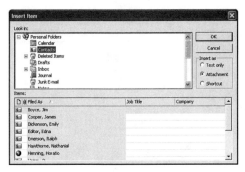

**Figure 3.33** The Insert Item dialog box.

## To insert an Outlook item:

1. Place the insertion point where you want to insert the item in the large text box.

2. Choose Insert > Item.

3. In the Insert Item dialog box, select the item that you want to insert (**Figure 3.33**):
   - ▲ In the Look In list, select the Outlook folder.
   - ▲ In the Items list, select the specific item in that folder.
   - ▲ In the Insert As area, select an option button to specify the way you want the item to be inserted.

4. Click the OK button.

## ✔ Tips

- You can also insert an item by opening its folder in Outlook and then dragging the item from the Outlook window and dropping it in the text box in the form.

- A quick way to create an email message and insert an Outlook item as an attachment is to select the item and choose Actions > Forward or press Ctrl+F. (For a contact, choose Actions > Forward As vCard.)

INSERTING FILES, ITEMS, AND OBJECTS

## To insert a linked or embedded object:

1. Place the insertion point where you want to insert the linked or embedded object in the large text box.

2. Choose Insert > Object.

   Outlook will display the Object dialog box.

3. To insert a linked object, select the Create from File tab, check the Link to File check box, and click the Browse button to select the file containing the data you want to link (**Figure 3.34**).

4. To insert an embedded object, select the Create New option button and select the type of object you want to embed in the Object Type list (**Figure 3.35**).

   After you click OK (in step 5), the source program will run and will let you create a new object. For example, if you selected the Bitmap Image object type, a bitmap window would open and would let you create a bitmap image.

   *or*

   Select the Create from File option button, leave the Link check box unchecked, and click the Browse button to select the file that contains the existing data you want to embed (**Figure 3.36**).

5. Click the OK button in the Insert Object dialog box.

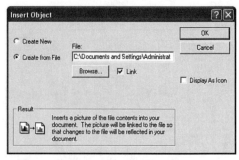

**Figure 3.34** Inserting a linked object. In this example, the object will be linked to an Excel workbook.

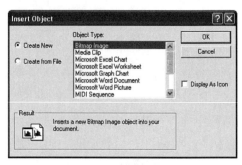

**Figure 3.35** Inserting an embedded object. In this example, a new object will be created in the Microsoft Clip Gallery program.

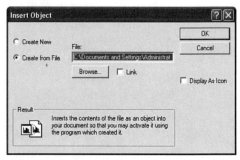

**Figure 3.36** Inserting an embedded object. In this example, the object will come from the existing data in an Excel workbook.

INSERTING FILES, ITEMS, AND OBJECTS

## ✔ Tips

- If you want to display an icon representing the linked or embedded object, rather than displaying the data itself, check the Display As Icon check box in the Insert Object dialog box.

- To edit a block of linked or embedded data, double-click it. (If this doesn't work for an embedded object, click on the object and choose Edit > Object Name Object, where Object Name is the name of the particular object, such as Worksheet.)

- To modify the properties of an embedded or linked object, right-click it and choose from the pop-up menu.

# Copying and Moving Items

The following are some ways in which you might want to copy or move an Outlook item:

◆ You can make a copy of an item in the same folder as the original to get a head start in creating a similar new item. For example, if you want to create a new item in your Contacts folder for a person who has the same address and phone number as an existing contact, you could make a copy of the existing contact and quickly edit it.

◆ You can copy an item to a different folder of the same type to create a backup. For example, you might make copies of your important incoming email messages in a separate mail-item folder for safe keeping.

◆ You can move items to different folders of the same type to organize your Outlook information. For example, to organize the messages you receive, you might move them from the Inbox to various mail-item folders, perhaps named Business Email and Personal Email.

◆ You can copy an item to a folder of a different type to get a head start in creating a new item based on the existing item. As explained in a tip earlier in the chapter (under "To create an item"), when you copy an item to a folder of a different type, Outlook creates a new item in the target folder that contains information from the existing item. For example, you could copy an incoming email message to your Contacts folder to create a new contact that already contains the name and email address of the person who sent you the message.

## ✔ Tip

■ See Chapter 4 for instructions on creating new folders.

**Figure 3.37** Copying an item to the Saved E-Mail folder.

## To copy or move an item:

1. Open the folder containing the item you want to copy or move, and select the item in the Outlook window. If you wish, you can select several items to copy or move them all at once.

2. To copy the item, choose Edit > Copy To Folder.

   *or*

   To move the item, choose Edit > Move To Folder or press Ctrl+Shift+V.

3. In the Copy Items dialog box (if you're copying) or in the Move Items dialog box (if you're moving), select the destination folder (**Figure 3.37**).

   If you want to create a new folder in which to store the copied or moved item, click the New button and specify the folder name, type, and location (as explained in Chapter 4).

4. Click the OK button.

   *or*

   ◆ To copy an item, hold down the Ctrl key and drag the item from the Information Viewer in the Outlook window and drop it on the Outlook Bar shortcut for the destination folder. If the shortcut isn't currently visible, while you drag, hold the item over the top or bottom of the current group to scroll through the shortcuts in that group, or hold it over the button for another group to open that group. (Keep the mouse button pressed the whole time!)

   ◆ To move an item, drag it the same way, but without pressing the Ctrl key.

   *Or*

*continues on next page*

**COPYING AND MOVING ITEMS**

1. Open the folder containing the item you want to copy or move and select the item in the Outlook window.

   If you wish, you can select several items and copy or move them all at once.

2. To copy the item, choose Edit > Copy or press Ctrl+C.

   *or*

   To move the item, choose Edit > Cut or press Ctrl+X.

3. Open the destination folder, and choose Edit > Paste or press Ctrl+V.

**Figure 3.38** Moving an item to a folder using the Move To Folder toolbar button.

## ✔ Tips

- You can also move an item by selecting it in the Outlook window, clicking the Move To Folder button on the Standard toolbar, and choosing one of the folders you've recently copied or moved an item to (**Figure 3.38**), or by choosing Move To Folder to open the Move Items dialog box (the same dialog box opened by choosing Edit > Move To Folder).

- If you've opened an item in a form, you can copy or move it to a different folder by choosing File > Copy To Folder or File > Move To Folder in the form (or by pressing Ctrl+Shift+V to move). These commands work just like the identically named commands on the Edit menu in the Outlook window.

- You can reverse an item copy or move operation by immediately clicking the Undo button on the Advanced toolbar, or by choosing Edit > Undo Copy or Edit > Undo Move, or by pressing Ctrl+Z. If you immediately reissue the Undo command, the copy or move will be restored.

**Figure 3.39** Selecting several Contacts items prior to deleting them.

# Removing and Archiving Items

When you remove an item from an Outlook folder, Outlook initially moves it to the Deleted Items folder rather than permanently deleting it. As long as the item remains in Deleted Items, you can easily recover it. You can permanently delete a removed item by removing it from Deleted Items; you will then no longer be able to recover it (unless you've made a backup copy somewhere else).

You can use the Outlook archiving feature to permanently delete items older than a specified period of time. You can also use the archiving feature to move your older items to an archive file, so that they'll be out of the way but yet you'll be able to recover them. You can set up the archive feature to run automatically at specified intervals, or you can run it manually at any time.

### To remove an Outlook item:

1. Select the item in the Outlook window. You can select several items to remove all of them (**Figure 3.39**).

2. Press Delete or Ctrl+D, click the Delete button on the Standard toolbar, or choose Edit > Delete.

   Outlook will then move the item to your Deleted Items folder.

   *or*

   If the item is opened in a form, click the Delete button on the form's Standard toolbar, choose File > Delete, or press Ctrl+D. (Some forms don't have all of these commands.)

   Outlook will then move the item to your Deleted Items folder.

## ✔ Tips

- You can restore an item you've removed by immediately clicking the Undo button on the Advanced toolbar, choosing Edit > Undo Delete, or pressing Ctrl+Z. (Immediately reissuing this command removes the item again.)

- As long as an item remains in the Deleted Items folder, you can recover it by simply moving the item from Deleted Items back to its original folder, using any of the methods described in "Copying and Moving Items," earlier in the chapter.

- You can permanently delete an item by removing it from the Deleted Items folder, using any of the methods explained in "To remove an Outlook item," earlier in the chapter.

- Outlook will warn you when you attempt to remove an item from Deleted Items and will give you the chance to cancel the deletion (**Figure 3.40**), provided that the Warn Before Permanently Deleting Items option is checked. To access this option, choose Tools > Options, open the Other tab, and click the Advanced Options button. To delete an item permanently, bypassing the Deleted Items folder, hold down the Shift key and press Delete to delete the item.

- You can remove all items from the Deleted Items folder—thereby permanently deleting them—by choosing Tools > Empty "Deleted Items" Folder. Outlook will display a warning and let you cancel the deletion (**Figure 3.41**). I recommend avoiding this command and using archiving instead to remove only your older items.

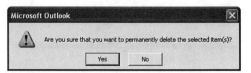

**Figure 3.40** Outlook's warning before it removes an item from Deleted Items.

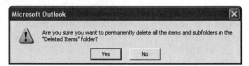

**Figure 3.41** Outlook's warning before it removes all items from Deleted Items.

REMOVING AND ARCHIVING ITEMS

- Outlook will remove all items from Deleted Items whenever you exit the program if the Empty the Deleted Items Folder Upon Exiting option is checked. To access this option, choose Tools > Options and open the Other tab. I recommend that you leave this option off, so that you'll have more time in which you can recover any removed items.

- You can also have the Outlook archive feature (described next) permanently delete items that are older than a certain time period. You can have it delete items from Deleted Items or directly from other folders.

- If you're using Outlook with Microsoft Exchange Server and are storing your files in a mailbox on the server, the server might delete older items from your Deleted Items folder.

**REMOVING AND ARCHIVING ITEMS**

## To archive automatically:

1. For each folder that you want to archive, right-click the folder's icon in the Outlook Bar, choose Properties on the pop-up menu, open the AutoArchive tab in the "Folder Name" Properties dialog box (where "Folder Name" represents the folder that you want to archive) (**Figure 3.42**), and select the desired options. Here are the options you can select:

   ▲ To enable automatic archiving for this folder, check Clean Out Items Older Than and specify a time period in the following text box and list box.

   ▲ To have old items removed from the folder but saved in an archive (.PST) file on your disk, select Move Old Items To and specify an archive (.PST) file in the following text box or just accept the default filename and location. I recommend selecting this option for all folders except Deleted Items, because you'll later be able to recover any archived item.

   ▲ To have old items removed from the folder and discarded, select Permanently Delete Old Items. I recommend selecting this option only for your Deleted Items folder, because it's unlikely that you'll need to recover any of these items.

2. Click the OK button.

3. Choose Tools > Options, open the Other tab, and click the AutoArchive button to open the AutoArchive dialog box (**Figure 3.43**).

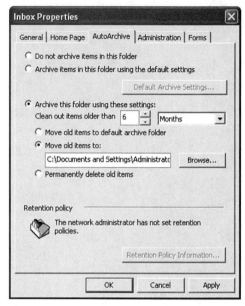

**Figure 3.42** The AutoArchive tab in the Inbox Properties dialog box.

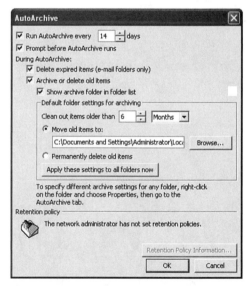

**Figure 3.43** The AutoArchive dialog box.

REMOVING AND ARCHIVING ITEMS

**4.** In the AutoArchive dialog box, select options as desired. Here are the options you can select:

▲ To enable automatic archiving, check Run AutoArchive Every and enter a number of days in the following text box to indicate the archiving frequency.

▲ Check Prompt Before AutoArchive Runs if you want to be able to choose whether or not to perform each scheduled archiving.

▲ Check Delete Expired Items... to have Outlook delete—rather than archive—expired email messages in mail-item folders when it performs automatic archiving (as you'll learn in Chapter 6, a message can be assigned an expiration date).

▲ Specify a default archive (.PST) file in the Default archive file text box, or just accept the current filename and location. Outlook will move all archived items to that file, except items in folders for which you have specified a different archive file (in step 1).

*or*

Select Permanently Delete Old Items to have the old items deleted instead of moved to an archive file. Choose Apply these setting to all folders now to set all folders to the current configuration.

▲ Retention policy gives a network administrator the ability to set retention policies that will override your local settings.

**5.** Click the OK button.

Outlook will automatically archive all folders for which you have enabled archiving (in step 1).

*continues on next page*

REMOVING AND ARCHIVING ITEMS

## ✔ Tips

- You can't enable automatic archiving for your Contacts folder. Outlook doesn't automatically archive Contacts items because they don't usually become obsolete with time, as messages, appointments, and other types of items do.

- You can prevent an individual item from being archived when its folder is automatically archived. To do this, open the item in a form, choose File > Properties in the form, and in the "Item Name" Properties dialog box ("Item Name" represents the name of the item), check Do Not AutoArchive This Item (**Figure 3.44**).

- To recover an archived item, choose File > Open > Outlook Data File (.pst) and select the archive file in the Open Personal Folders dialog box. Outlook will then open the archive file and display its folders in the Folder List. You can use the Folder List to open the folder containing the archived item, and copy the item back to its original folder.

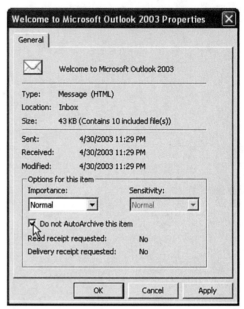

**Figure 3.44** Checking the Do not AutoArchive This Item property.

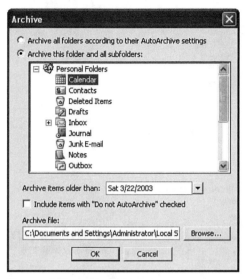

Figure 3.45 The Archive dialog box.

## To archive manually:

1. Choose File > Archive to open the Archive dialog box (**Figure 3.45**).

2. Select options as desired in the Archive dialog box:

   ▲ Select Archive All Folders According to Their AutoArchive Settings to have Outlook archive just as if an automatic archiving session were running, using the settings described in the previous section, "To archive automatically." If you select this option, the other options in the Archive dialog box will have no effect.

   ▲ To manually archive a specific folder and its subfolders, select Archive This Folder and All Subfolders and select the folder in the following list.

   ▲ Enter the archive date into the Archive Items Older Than box (click the down-arrow to display a calendar). Only items older than the date you specify will be archived.

   ▲ Normally, you can prevent an individual item from being archived by opening the item in a form, choosing File > Properties in the form, and checking Do Not AutoArchive This Item. However, you can have Outlook archive items regardless of this setting by checking Include Items With "Do Not AutoArchive" Checked.

   ▲ Specify the archive (.PST) file in the Archive File text box, or accept the default filename and location.

3. Click the OK button.

# Using Different Views

When you've opened an Outlook folder, you can change the overall way you view and work with the information it displays by switching to a different view. Each type of Outlook folder provides a unique set of views, designed specifically for working with the items it contains.

For example, in the Contacts folder you can select the Address Cards view to display each item in a format that resembles a business card (**Figure 3.46**). You can select the Phone List view to display all items in a table, where each row displays a different contact and each column displays a particular field of information (such as the name or company) for all contacts (**Figure 3.47**). Or, you can select the By Category view to display all items in a table where the items are grouped according to their categories (**Figure 3.48**).

## ✔ Tips

■ As you'll learn later in the book, you can assign one or more categories to any type of Outlook item. Categories can be used for sorting, filtering, grouping, or finding items.

■ In the "Adjusting Views" section in Chapter 14, "Customizing Outlook," you'll learn how to modify a standard view (such as those shown in **Figures 3.46 through 3.48**), as well as how to create a new custom view.

**Figure 3.46** The Contacts folder in the Address Cards view.

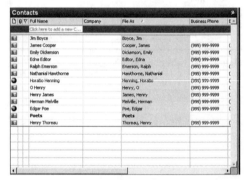

**Figure 3.47** The Contacts folder in the Phone List view.

**Figure 3.48** The Contacts folder in the By Category view.

USING DIFFERENT VIEWS

**Figure 3.49** Select a view in the Current View list box on the Advanced toolbar.

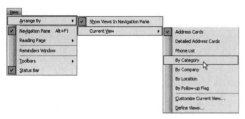

**Figure 3.50** Choose view from the Current View submenu.

*Column header*

*Drag right edge to adjust column width*

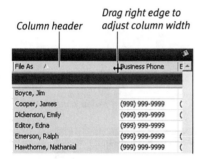

**Figure 3.51** Adjust the width of the File As column in a table view.

## To change the view:

◆ Click the down-arrow on the Current View list box on the Advanced toolbar, and select a new view in the list by clicking on it (**Figure 3.49**).

*or*

Choose View > Arrange By > Current View, and then choose a view from the submenu (**Figure 3.50**).

## ✔ Tips

■ In a table view (a view with rows and columns such as the Phone List view shown in **Figure 3.47**), you can adjust the width of a column by dragging the right edge of the header above that column to the right or left (**Figure 3.51**). You can also quickly adjust the width to exactly fit the column's contents by double-clicking the right edge of the header, or by right-clicking anywhere on the header and choosing Best Fit from the pop-up menu.

■ Choose View > Arrange By > Show Views In Navigation Pane to display at the bottom of the Navigation Pane the views available.

# Displaying the Reading Pane

With any view, you can display a Reading pane at the right or bottom of the Information Viewer in the Outlook window. The main area of the Preview pane displays the contents of the large text box of the selected item (or the entire contents of a Notes item), and the header displays selected item fields (**Figure 3.52**).

### To display the Reading pane:

1. Activate the view in which you want to display the Reading pane.

2. Click the Reading Pane button on the Advanced toolbar, or select View > Reading Pane and choose Right, Bottom, or Off.

   If you click the button or choose Off in the menu command, the Reading pane will be hidden.

*Header*                                    *Preview pane*

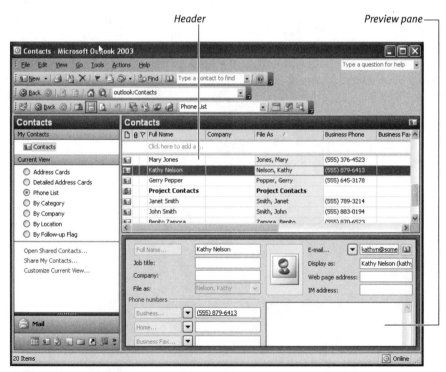

**Figure 3.52** The Reading pane displayed in the Address Cards view of the Contacts folder.

*Drag up or down to adjust pane height*

**Figure 3.53** Adjusting the height of the Reading pane by dragging the top edge.

*Drag right or left to adjust pane width*

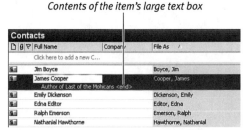

**Figure 3.54** Redisplaying the Reading pane header by dragging the left edge.

*Contents of the item's large text box*

**Figure 3.55** A Contacts item with AutoPreview on, showing the contents of the large text box.

## ✔ Tips

- Once you display the Reading pane in a particular view, it will always be displayed whenever that view is active, until you explicitly turn off the Reading pane in the view.

- You can adjust the height of the Reading pane by dragging its top border up or down (**Figure 3.53**) or right to left (**Figure 3.54**) depending on the view.

- In a table view (a view with rows and columns such as the Phone List view shown in **Figure 3.47**), you can display the first part of the text contained in the item's large text box, right below each item (**Figure 3.55**). To do this, click the AutoPreview button on the Advanced toolbar or choose View > AutoPreview. Reissuing this command turns off the preview display.

- You can modify features of the Reading pane—such as Mark Item as Read When Selection Changes—by choosing Tools > Options, opening the Other tab, and clicking the Reading Pane button.

**USING DIFFERENT VIEWS**

# Sorting, Filtering, and Grouping Items

You can control the way Outlook displays the items in a particular view in three ways:

◆ **Sorting**, which means changing the order in which items are displayed. You can sort using up to four different item fields. For example, using three fields, you could sort your email messages by the senders' names, with all messages from the same sender sorted by date, and all messages sent on the same date sorted by subject.

◆ **Filtering**, which means limiting the items that are displayed. For example, you could filter your Contacts items so that only contacts from your home town are shown.

◆ **Grouping**, which means dividing the items into separate sets, where all the items in a set have the same value in a particular field. For example, if you grouped tasks using the Priority field, all tasks in each group would have the same priority value (low, normal, or high). You can have groups within groups, using as many as four fields. For example, using two fields, you could group your tasks by priority, with the items within each priority group grouped by status (not started, in progress, and so on). Grouping is like sorting, but the different sets are labeled with headers and you can individually expand or collapse them.

**Figure 3.56** shows the Phone List view of the Contacts folder, with the default settings—that is, before sorting, filtering, or grouping is applied. Notice that the items are sorted by the File As field (usually the last name followed by the first name), all items in the folder are shown, and the items aren't grouped. In the following instructions, you'll see the effects of applying sorting, filtering, and grouping to this view.

**Figure 3.56** The Phone List view of the Contacts folder, before sorting, filtering, or grouping has been applied.

## ✔ Tips

■ You apply sorting, filtering, and grouping to a particular view. Each view of a folder can have different sorting, filtering, or grouping settings.

■ The availability of sorting, filtering, and grouping depends upon the particular view. For example, you can apply grouping only to a table view (such as the Phone List view shown in **Figure 3.56**) or a time-line view (such as Task Timeline view of the Tasks folder). Also, you can't apply any of these settings to the Day/Week/Month view of the Calendar folder.

**Figure 3.57** Right-clicking a blank area to display the pop-up menu.

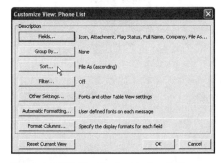

**Figure 3.58** Clicking the Sort button in the View Summary dialog box.

**Figure 3.59** The Sort dialog box.

## To sort items:

1. Activate the view in which you want to set the sorting order of the items.

2. Right-click a blank area (not on an item!) in the Information Viewer (**Figure 3.57**), and choose Sort from the pop-up menu.

   *or*

   If you can't find a blank spot, choose View > Arrange By > Current View > Customize Current View, and click the Sort button in the View Summary dialog box (**Figure 3.58**).

3. In the Sort dialog box (**Figure 3.59**), specify the primary sorting criterion by selecting the field you want to use for sorting in the Sort Items By list box and selecting either an Ascending or Descending sort.

4. If you want to sort using additional fields, specify each one in a Then By area of the Sort dialog box.

   *continues on next page*

**5.** Click the OK button.

**Figure 3.60** shows the Phone List view of the Contacts folder after an ascending sort using the Full Name field has been applied (as shown in **Figure 3.59**), which sorts the items by first name.

## ✔ Tips

- In the Sort dialog box, you can change the fields that are available for sorting by selecting an item in the Select Available Fields From list box.

- You can't sort items in a time-based view, such as the Task Timeline view of the Task folder or the Day/Week/Month view of the Calendar folder.

- In a table view, you can quickly sort the items using a particular field by clicking the corresponding column header (**Figure 3.61**). Subsequent clicks toggle between an ascending sort (indicated with an up-pointing triangle in the header) and a descending sort (indicated with a down-pointing triangle). To use one or more additional fields for sorting, click each header while pressing Shift; Outlook will use the fields in the order you click them.

- If a column header is too narrow, you won't see the triangle indicating that the field is being used for sorting.

**Figure 3.60** The Phone List view of the Contacts folder, sorted by Full Name.

*Indicates an ascending sort using this field*

**Figure 3.61** Sorting by the File As field by clicking the column header.

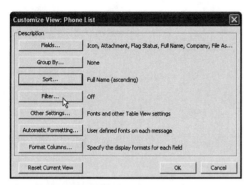

**Figure 3.62** Clicking the Filter button in the View Summary dialog box.

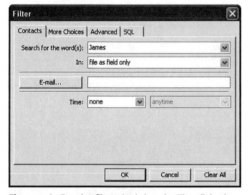

**Figure 3.63** Entering filter criteria into the Filter dialog box.

**Figure 3.64** The effect of applying the filter criteria shown in Figure 3.62 to the Phone List view.

## To filter items:

1. Activate the view in which you want to filter the items.

2. Right-click a blank area (not on an item!) in the Information Viewer (see **Figure 3.57**), and choose Filter from the pop-up menu.

   *or*

   If you can't find a blank spot, choose View > Arrange By > Current View > Customize Current View and click the Filter button in the View Summary dialog box (**Figure 3.62**).

3. Select the filter criteria in the tabs of the Filter dialog box.

   For example, if you typed the name **James** in the Search for the Word(s) text box and selected File as Field Only in the In list box (**Figure 3.63**), Outlook would display only the items that have the word "James" in the File As field (**Figure 3.64**).

4. Click the OK button.

## ✔ Tips

- The Filter dialog box displays the same tabs and controls as the Advanced Find dialog box, described later in the chapter, with the SQL tab the only addition.

- When the items in the current view are filtered, the message "Filter Applied" appears both on the right end of the Folder Banner and on the left end of the Status bar (see **Figure 3.64**), letting you know that not all items are displayed.

- To remove a filter and display all items, reopen the Filter dialog box, as explained in step 2 above, click the Clear All button, and then click the OK button.

**SORTING, FILTERING, AND GROUPING ITEMS**

## To group items:

1. Activate the view in which you want to group the items. You must activate a table view.

2. Right-click a blank area (not on an item!) in the Information Viewer (**Figure 3.57**), and choose Group By from the pop-up menu.

   *or*

   If you can't find a blank spot, choose View > Arrange By > Current View > Customize Current View and click the Group By button in the Customize View dialog box (**Figure 3.65**).

3. In the Group By dialog box (**Figure 3.66**), specify the primary grouping criterion by selecting the field you want to use for grouping in the Group Items By list box, and selecting either Ascending or Descending to set the order in which the groups are listed.

4. If you want groups within groups, specify each nested group in a Then By area of the Group By dialog box.

5. Select an option in the Expand/Collapse Defaults list box to specify how the groups will be shown when you first display the view.

6. Click the OK button.

As an example, the Group By dialog box settings shown in **Figure 3.67** would divide the items in the Phone List view of the Contacts folder as shown in **Figure 3.68**.

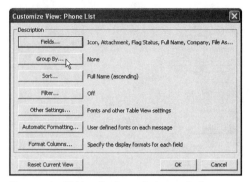

**Figure 3.65** Clicking the Group By button in the Customize View dialog box.

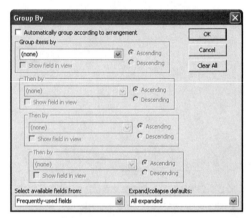

**Figure 3.66** The Group By dialog box.

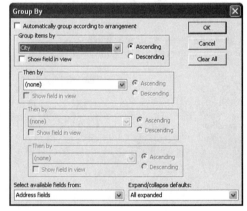

**Figure 3.67** Settings for grouping contacts by city.

**Figure 3.68** The result of the settings shown in Figure 3.66.

*Right-click here to open pop-up menu*

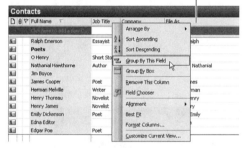

**Figure 3.69** Using the Categories field for grouping items.

## ✔ Tips

- In the Group By dialog box, you can change the fields that are available for grouping by selecting an item in the Select Available Fields From list box.

- A quick way to group items using a field that's displayed in a column of the Information Viewer is to right-click the column header and choose Group By This Field from the pop-up menu (**Figure 3.69**). Repeat this operation for any nested groups you wish to add; Outlook will group using the fields in the order in which you designate them.

- You can collapse or expand a group of items displayed in the Information Viewer by clicking the - (insert minus) or + (insert plus) button at the top of the group. You can collapse or expand all groups by choosing View > Expand/Collapse Groups > Collapse All or View > Expand/Collapse Groups > Expand All.

- Some standard views already have grouping applied. For example, the By Category view of the Contacts folder groups records using the Category field.

- To remove all grouping, open the Group By dialog box, as explained in step 2 on the previous page, click the Clear All button, and then click the OK button.

# Using the Organize Page

The Organize Page is a Web-style page that you can display in a pane at the top of the Information Viewer (**Figure 3.70**). It contains a set of controls that you can use to work with items in various ways. The particular controls that are available—and the things you can do in the Organize Page—depend upon the Outlook folder in which it's displayed. Here's an overall list of what you can do using the Organize Page:

◆ Switch views

◆ Move an item to a different folder

◆ Assign a category to an item or create a new category

◆ Automatically color-code messages

*Organize Page*

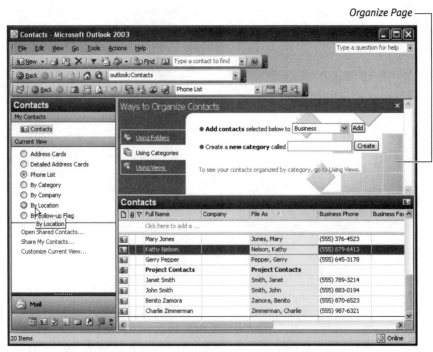

**Figure 3.70** The Organize Page displayed in the Active Appointments view of the Calendar folder.

*First, click a command category here...*

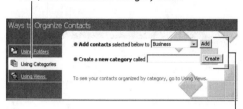

*...then, use the controls here to carry out a command*

**Figure 3.71** Using the Organize Page.

## ✔ Tips

- Moving messages and color-coding messages are described in "Organizing Your Messages with Rules" in Chapter 6.

- The Organize Page doesn't let you do anything you can't do through conventional program commands. However, it's sometimes easier to use than conventional commands.

## To use the Organize Page:

1. Open the folder containing the items you want to work with, and activate the desired view.

2. Choose Tools > Organize.
   Outlook will display the Organize Page (**Figure 3.70**).

3. Click the desired category of commands on the left side of the page.

4. Use the controls to issue the commands you want (**Figure 3.71**).

## ✔ Tips

- To remove the Organize Page, click the Close Organize button in the upper-right corner of the page.

- Search Folders are a good method for organizing and are described in Chapter 4's "Creating and Using Search Folders" section.

# Finding Outlook Items

Outlook provides the following search tools:

Find Bar

◆ The easiest way to locate Outlook items containing specific text is to use the **Find Bar**, which is a page that you can display in a bar at the top of the Information Viewer (**Figure 3.72**).

◆ To locate Outlook items using more exacting search criteria—for example, to search through more than one Outlook folder—you need to use the **Advanced Find dialog box** (**Figure 3.73**).

**Figure 3.72** The Find Bar displayed in the Contacts folder.

## To use the Find Bar:

1. Open the Outlook folder where you want to search for items.

2. Click the Find button on the Standard toolbar, or choose Tools > Find > Find. Outlook will display the Find Bar (**Figure 3.74**).

3. Type the text you want to search for in the Look For text box.

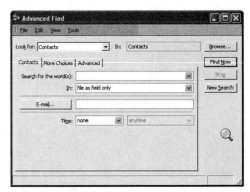

**Figure 3.73** The Advanced Find dialog box (searching for contacts).

Find button

**Figure 3.74** The Find Bar.

**Figure 3.75** Choose a selection from the Search In drop menu

**Figure 3.76** The Contacts folder after searching for all items that contain the text *james*.

**4.** Choose a selection from the Search In drop box (**Figure 3.75**).

**5.** Click the Find Now button.

Outlook will now display only those items—if there are any—that contain the text you typed (**Figure 3.76**).

**6.** If you didn't find the item you were looking for, you can click Options in the Find Bar and choose Advanced Find to display the Advanced Find dialog box (described next).

*or*

You can click Clear to restore the items that were displayed before you performed the search, and to empty the Look For list box so you can perform another search.

## ✔ Tips

■ For faster searches, you can uncheck Search All Text in Each Message in the Options drop-down list in the Find Bar, which causes Outlook to search only the most common item fields. If you don't find what you're looking for, you can then check Search All Text in Each Message to do a more thorough search.

■ To remove the Find Bar (and restore the display of all items, if you performed a search), click the Find button on the Standard toolbar again, or click the Close Find button in the upper-right corner of the page.

## To use the Advanced Find dialog box:

1. Choose Tools > Find > Advanced Find, or press Ctrl+Shift+F.

   *or*

   If you've displayed the Find Page, you can click the Advanced Find button by choosing Options > Advanced Find. (**Figure 3.77**)

   Outlook will open the Advanced Find dialog box (**Figure 3.78**). It doesn't matter which folder is open when you display this dialog box—you can always search for any kind of item or disk file in any Outlook or Exchange folder.

2. In the Look For list box in the Advanced Find dialog box, select the type of item or file you want to search for:

   ▲ Select Any Type of Outlook item to search for all types of items.

   ▲ Select a specific type of Outlook item (such as Messages, Contacts, or Journal entries) to narrow your search to just that type of item.

   ▲ Select Files (Outlook/Exchange) to search for disk files that are stored in Outlook or Exchange mail-item folders.

3. Click the Browse button to select one or more folders that you want to search (Outlook folders or Archive folders), or just accept the default folder displayed in the Inbox. (Outlook selects a default folder to be searched, based upon the type of item or file that you select in the Look For list box.)

4. Enter your search criteria into the tabs of the Advanced Find dialog box.

   The tabs you see and the controls they contain depend upon the type of item you are searching for. **Figures 3.73**, **3.76**, and **3.77** show the Advanced Find dialog box as it appears when you search for contacts, messages, and disk files.

**Figure 3.77** The Advanced Find dialog box (searching for messages).

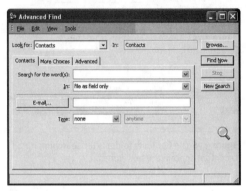

**Figure 3.78** The Advanced Find dialog box (searching for disk files).

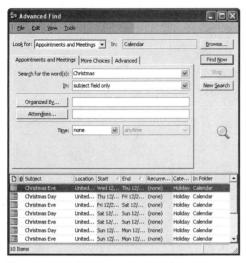

**Figure 3.79** The Advanced Find dialog box, after a search has been performed.

**5.** Click the Find Now button.

Outlook will then perform the search and will display the items or files it finds—if any—at the bottom of the Advanced Find dialog box. The items are displayed in the same way they would be displayed in the Outlook window. **Figure 3.79** shows search criteria entered into the Advanced Find dialog box with the results of the search displayed at the bottom.

### ✔ Tips

■ The Advanced Find dialog box provides many of the same commands as the Outlook window for sorting, grouping, changing the view, or customizing the view.

■ You can open or work with the items displayed in the Advanced Find dialog box using many of the techniques described in this chapter, working within the dialog box.

■ After you've entered a set of search criteria into the Advanced Find dialog box (which might be fairly involved), you can save your criteria by choosing File > Save Search in the dialog box. If you later want to perform the same search again, you can retrieve your saved search criteria by choosing File > Open Search.

■ You can use the Advanced Find dialog box even if you aren't running Outlook! To display it, choose Search > Using Microsoft Outlook on your Windows Start menu (opened by clicking the Start button on the Windows taskbar).

# WORKING WITH OUTLOOK FOLDERS

4

As explained in Chapter 2, Outlook folders are the places where information is stored, displayed, and managed. When you set up Outlook, it creates a default set of folders, one for each basic type of information that it manages. As you begin working with Outlook and organizing your personal information, however, you'll soon want to start adding, rearranging, or renaming folders, just as you would if you were storing information in a file cabinet.

In Chapter 2, you learned different ways to locate and open an Outlook folder. In this chapter, you'll learn how to

- ◆ Create new folders
- ◆ Move or copy folders
- ◆ Rename folders
- ◆ Remove folders
- ◆ Share folders over a network (Exchange Server)
- ◆ Create and use Search Folders
- ◆ Print folders
- ◆ Change folder properties

# Creating New Folders

You might want to create one or more new Outlook folders for a variety of reasons. For example, you might want to do the following:

◆ Create one or more additional mail-item folders for storing and organizing the messages you've received—perhaps one folder for personal email messages, one for business email messages, and one for newsletters or discussion list messages.

◆ Create an additional calendar-item folder so that you can keep your personal appointments in one folder and your business appointments and meetings in another.

◆ Create a task-item folder for each major project that you're managing.

◆ Create a new folder in the Public Folders area on the server to use for sharing information with other people on your network (Exchange Server).

## ✔ Tips

■ Outlook folders are organized in a hierarchy. That is, folders can contain other folders, as well as items. A single root folder at the top of the hierarchy is named either Personal folders or Mailbox, depending on where the folders are stored, and contains all other folders (**Figure 4.1**).

■ When you create a new Outlook folder, you can place it within any other Outlook folder, making it a subfolder of the original folder.

**Figure 4.1** The hierarchy of the default Outlook folders.

**Figure 4.2** The Create New Folder dialog box.

## To create a new folder:

1. Choose File > Folder > New Folder, or press Ctrl+Shift+E.

   Outlook opens the Create New Folder dialog box (**Figure 4.2**).

2. In the Name text box, enter a name for your new folder.

3. In the Folder Contains list box, select the type of items you want to store in your new folder:

   ▲ **Calendar items** are appointments, events, or meetings. These are the item types that are stored in the default Calendar folder.

   ▲ **Contact Items** are contacts (descriptions of your personal or business contacts) or distribution lists (sets of contacts). This is the item type that is stored in the default Contacts folder.

   ▲ **Journal Items** are journal entries (records of events that have occurred). This is the item type that is stored in the default Journal folder.

   ▲ **Mail and Post Items** are email messages, fax messages, and other items. This is the item type that is stored in the default Inbox, Drafts, Outbox, and Saved Items folders.

   ▲ **Note Items** are text notes that you jot down. This is the item type that is stored in the default Notes folder.

   ▲ **Task Items** are tasks (descriptions of jobs or projects you need to complete). This is the item type that is stored in the default Tasks folder.

   *continues on next page*

CREATING NEW FOLDERS

**4.** In the Select Where to Place the Folder list, select (click on) the folder in which you want to store your new folder.

Your new folder will become a subfolder of the selected folder. If necessary, click the + symbol to expand the branch of the hierarchy that contains the folder you want to select. **Figure 4.3** shows an example of a completed Create New Folder dialog box.

**5.** Click the OK button.

## ✔ Tips

■ If you opt not to create a shortcut for your new folder, you can open it using the Folder List, as described in "To open a folder using the Folder List" in Chapter 2. You can also create a shortcut later, using the method outlined in "Modifying the Navigation Pane" in Chapter 14, "Customizing Outlook."

■ You can get a head start in creating a new folder that's similar to an existing one by making a copy of the existing folder. Instructions are given in the next section.

**Figure 4.3** Settings for creating a new folder for saving email messages. The folder will be named Saved E-Mail and will be located within the default Inbox folder.

*Before moving*

**Figure 4.4** The folder hierarchy *before* moving Saved Business E-Mail and Saved Personal E-Mail.

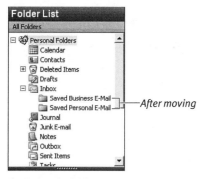

*After moving*

**Figure 4.5** The folder hierarchy *after* moving Saved Business E-Mail and Saved Personal E-Mail to the Inbox folder.

# Moving and Copying Folders

You can move a folder from its current position in the Outlook folder hierarchy to another position. Doing so can help you organize your Outlook folders, just as you might move a paper file folder to a different file drawer.

For example, if you created several folders for storing email messages and you initially made them subfolders of Outlook Today (like all of the default Outlook folders), you might later decide to move them to your Inbox (making them subfolders of Inbox), so that all your new email folders would be grouped in a single location (see **Figures 4.4** and **4.5**).

You can also make a copy of an Outlook folder, placing the copy in the same folder as the original or in a different folder.

For example, you might make a backup copy of your Sent Items folder for safekeeping. Or, if you wanted to create a separate calendar-item folder for your personal appointments, you could make a copy of your Calendar folder—rather than creating a new folder—so you wouldn't have to reenter information already contained in Calendar.

## ✔ Tips

■ You can't move a default Outlook folder (Inbox, Calendar, and so on), although you can make a copy of it.

■ When you move or copy a folder, you also move or copy all items contained in the folder.

## To move or copy a folder:

1. Open the folder you want to move or copy.

2. To move the folder, chose File > Folder > Move "Folder," where Folder is the name of the currently opened folder (such as Saved E-Mail).

   *or*

   To copy the folder, choose File > Folder > Copy "Folder."

   Outlook will open the Move Folder dialog box (**Figure 4.6**) or the Copy Folder dialog box (**Figure 4.7**).

3. In the dialog box, select the folder in which you want to store the moved or copied folder. If necessary, click the + symbol to open the branch of the folder hierarchy containing the target folder.

4. Click the OK button.

## ✔ Tips

- In the Folder List (see "To open a folder using the Folder List" in Chapter 2), you can right-click any folder in the list and choose Move "Folder" or Copy "Folder" from the pop-up menu to move or copy that folder, without having to first open the folder (**Figure 4.8**).

- In the Folder List, you can also quickly move a folder by dragging it to the destination folder. To copy the folder, press Ctrl while you drag.

- In the next section, you'll learn how to assign a different name to your moved or copied folder.

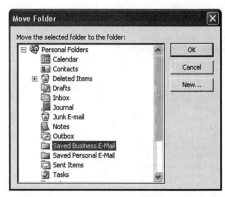

**Figure 4.6** The Move Folder dialog box.

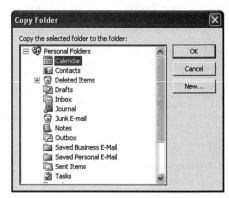

**Figure 4.7** The Copy Folder dialog box.

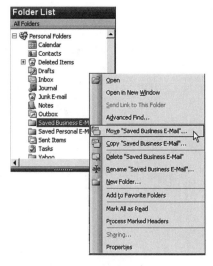

**Figure 4.8** Using the pop-up menu in the Folder List to move a folder.

**Figure 4.9** The Rename dialog box.

*Type a new name in this box*

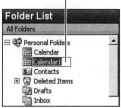

**Figure 4. 10** Editing a folder name in the Folder List.

# Renaming Folders

You can rename any Outlook folder that you have created. (You can't rename a default Outlook folder, such as Inbox or Calendar, however.)

For example, if you have made a copy of the Calendar folder in the same folder as the original, Outlook will name the copy Calendar1. You'll probably want to give it a more descriptive name, such as Business Schedule or Personal Appointments.

### To rename a folder:

1. Open the folder you want to rename.

2. Choose File > Folder > Rename "Folder," where Folder is the name of the currently opened folder.

   Outlook will display the Rename dialog box (**Figure 4.9**).

3. Type the name you want into the New Name text box.

4. Click the OK button.

### ✔ Tip

- In the Folder List, you can rename any folder that you've created (without first opening the folder), by right-clicking the folder in the list and choosing Rename "Folder" from the pop-up menu. Outlook highlights the folder name in the Folder List and lest you edit the name in place (**Figure 4.10**).

# Removing Folders

You can remove any Outlook folder that you have created. (You can't remove a default Outlook folder, such as Inbox or Calendar, however.) When you remove a folder, Outlook initially moves the folder and all its contents to the Deleted Items folder. As long as the folder remains in Deleted Items, you can easily recover it. If it gets permanently deleted from Deleted Items, you'll no longer be able to recover it.

### To remove a folder:

1. Open the folder you want to remove.

2. Choose File > Folder > Delete "Folder," where Folder is the name of the currently opened folder (**Figure 4.11**).

   Outlook will warn you before deleting the folder (**Figure 4.12**).

3. Click Yes in the warning dialog box to proceed with the deletion.

### ✔ Tips

■ You can delete from the Folder List any folder that you've created (without first opening the folder) by right-clicking the folder in the list and choosing Delete "Folder" from the pop-up menu. Or, you can simply click the folder and press the Delete key.

■ To recover a removed folder that's still in Deleted Items, simply move it from Deleted Items back to its original location.

■ To permanently delete a removed folder, remove it from Deleted Items. To do this, you can use any of the methods provided in this section or any of the methods for permanently removing an item that are presented in "To permanently delete a removed item" in Chapter 3, "Working with Outlook Items."

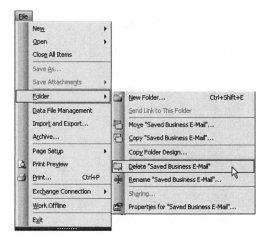

**Figure 4.11** Choosing the menu command for deleting the opened folder.

**Figure 4.12** The warning message Outlook displays before deleting a folder.

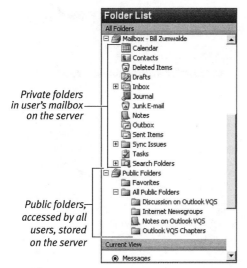

Private folders
in user's mailbox
on the server

Public folders,
accessed by all
users, stored
on the server

**Figure 4.13** The folder List for an Exchange Server user.

# Sharing Folders over a Network

If you're using Outlook with Microsoft Exchange Server, you can share Outlook folders with other Outlook users on the network in either of the following ways:

◆ You can share a private folder with one or more specific users, or with all users. A private folder is one that is stored in your mailbox on the server. Exchange Server creates a personal mailbox for each user on the network. It's the usual location for your default Outlook folders (Inbox, Calendar, Contacts, and so on), as well as the folders you create to store your personal information.

◆ You can create a public folder, which is stored in the Public Folders area of the server.

Exchange Server provides a single Public Folders area on the server, although an Exchange administrator can add others. All users can easily access folders in the Public Folders area using the Folder List or shortcuts (although, if desired, the folder creator can limit access).

**Figure 4.13** shows the Folder List for a setup in which Outlook is being used with Exchange Server. Notice that the default Outlook folders (including Inbox, where email messages are delivered) are all private folders located in the user's mailbox on the server. Two additional folders are stored in a Personal Folders (.PST) file on the user's hard disk. The Public Folders are stored on the server and are shared by all Outlook users on the network.

## To share a private folder:

1. Open the folder you want to share. It must be a private folder in your mailbox.

2. Choose File > Folder > Properties For "Folder" (where Folder is the name of the currently opened folder) and open the Permissions tab (**Figure 4.14**).

3. To share the folder with everyone on the network, assign the desired permission level to the Default user by selecting that user in the list and selecting the desired permission level in the Permission Level list box.

   Initially, the Default user is assigned the None level of permission, which denies sharing. When you select a permission level, the options for that level are automatically selected in the Permissions area. If you want to create a custom level of permission, you can select individual options in this area.

4. To share the folder with one or more specific users, click the Add button, select the users in the Add Users dialog box (**Figure 4.15**), and click OK. Then, in the Permissions tab assign the desired permission level to each user.

5. Click OK in the Properties dialog box.

## ✔ Tips

■ You can open the Properties dialog box for any folder, without first opening that folder, by right-clicking the folder in the Folder List and then choosing Properties from the pop-up menu.

■ Outlook items that have the Private option checked won't be shared with others. (In later chapters, you'll learn about checking this option.)

■ The permissions assigned to Anonymous in the Permissions tab determine the actions that users outside your domain can perform with a folder.

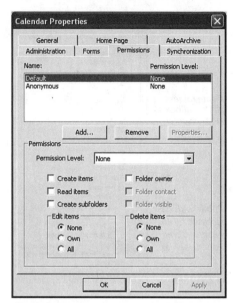

**Figure 4.14** The Permissions tab of the Calendar Properties dialog box.

**Figure 4.15** The Add Users dialog box.

**Figure 4.16** The Open Other User's Folder dialog box.

**Figure 4.17** Creating a public folder.

## To access another user's shared private folder:

1. Choose File > Open > Other User's Folder. Outlook will open the Open Other User's Folder dialog box (**Figure 4.16**).

2. Type the user's name into the text box, or click the Name button to select the name from a list of Outlook users on the network.

3. Select the folder you want to access in the Folder list box.

4. Click the OK button.

Outlook will open the shared folder in a separate window. You can then view, open, or work with the items it contains, according to your level of permission.

## To create a public folder:

◆ Follow the instructions for creating a new folder given in the section "To create a new folder," earlier in the chapter. In step 4, simply place your new folder within All Public Folders in the Public Folders area, or within one of its subfolders (**Figure 4.17**).

## ✔ Tip

■ When you create a public folder, all other users are initially granted the Author level of permission, which lets them create items, read items, and edit or delete the items they create. You can change permissions in the Permissions tab of the folder's Properties dialog box. (For instructions on opening this tab, see "To change a folder's properties," later in the chapter.)

**SHARING FOLDERS OVER A NETWORK**

## To access a public folder:

◆ To open a public folder, use the Folder List, or click a shortcut if you've created one. (Creating shortcuts is discussed in "Modifying the Navigation Pane" in Chapter 14.)

◆ To work with the items in the folder, use the techniques discussed in Chapter 3.

◆ To work with the folder itself, use the techniques described in this chapter.

## ✔ Tips

■ If someone else has created the folder, your permission level, set by the folder creator, will determine which operations you can perform.

■ You can use a public folder that stores mail items to carry on a group discussion (much like a discussion on an online bulletin board). To post a new discussion item, choose File > New > Post In This Folder or press Ctrl+Shift+S. To reply to a discussion item, open it and click the Reply button on the form's Standard toolbar.

■ You can also share Office documents and other types of disk files by storing them in a public mail-item folder. To store a file, simply drag it from Windows Explorer or a file folder and drop it on the public folder name in the Folder List or on the folder's shortcut in the Navigation Pane. The file can be opened the same way you open a regular Outlook item.

■ To locate a public folder, choose Tools > Find > Find Public Folder and enter search criteria into the Find Public Folders dialog box (**Figure 4.18**).

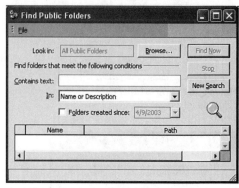

**Figure 4.18** The Find Public Folders dialog box.

**Figure 4.19** Examples of built-in Folders.

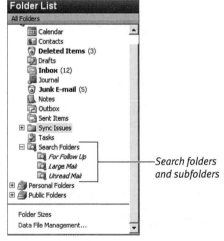

*Search folders and subfolders*

**Figure 4.20** Displaying built-in Search Folders.

# Creating and Using Search Folders

Outlook organizes items by using folders. Inbox, Sent Items, and Drafts are a few examples of built-in folders (**Figure 4.19**). Search Folders are virtual folders designed to display the results of search queries. They are different from physical folders in that they don't really exist as folders, but instead are really a type of view. Search folders enable you to automatically organize messages without creating message rules.

The three default Search folders for Mail are: For Follow Up (mail marked with a flag), Large Mail (mail larger than 100KB), and Unread Mail (**Figure 4.20**). Simply click on one of these folders in the Navigation pane to view its contents.

*continues on next page*

CREATING AND USING SEARCH FOLDERS

You can choose from a variety of search conditions when you create a search folder, enabling you to create search folders for specific tasks. This section focuses on a specific search folder use—displaying mail from specific senders.

### To create this search folder:

1. Open the Inbox (**Figure 4.21**).

2. Choose File > New > Search Folder (**Figure 4.22**).

3. In the New Search Folder dialog box, select Mail From Specific People from the Mail From People and Lists list and click Choose (**Figure 4.23**).

4. Choose the contacts whose messages you want to include in the folder (**Figure 4.24**).

5. Click the From button to add the contacts to the address list (**Figure 4.25**).

6. Click Ok to close the Select Names dialog box.

7. The selection(s) will be displayed in the Show Mail from These People box (**Figure 4.26**).

8. Click OK to complete the creation of the search folder.

The new Search Folder, created using steps 1-8, is displayed (**Figure 4.27**)

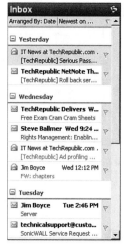

**Figure 4.21** The Inbox opened by clicking the Mail folder on the Navigation pane.

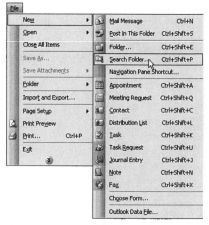

**Figure 4.22** Creating a new Search Folder.

**Figure 4.23** Selecting to search based on Mail from People and Lists.

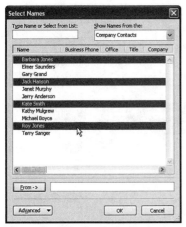

**Figure 4.24** Selecting the names to include in the Search Folder.

**Figure 4.25** Clicking the From button to add the names.

**Figure 4.26** Displaying the selected people in the Show Mail from These People box.

## ✔ Tips

- Right-click on Search Folder in the Folder List and choose New Search Folder to quickly create a folder (**Figure 4.28**).

- Select more than one contact by holding the Ctrl button and clicking on the desired selections in the Select Names dialog box. Then, click From to add them to the address list (**Figure 4.24**).

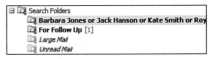

**Figure 4.27** A completed Search Folder.

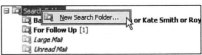

**Figure 4.28** Right-click on Search Folder to quickly create a folder.

## To delete a search folder

1. Select the Search Folder you want to delete (**Figure 4.29**).

2. Choose Edit > Delete (**Figure 4.30**).

   *or*

   Press Ctrl+D.

   *or*

   Right-click on the folder and choose Delete "Folder," where Folder is the name of the folder.

3. The Microsoft Outlook dialog box is displayed asking you if you're sure that you want to permanently delete the Search Folder (**Figure 4.31**).

   Note that deleting the virtual Search Folder will not delete the items from their original folders.

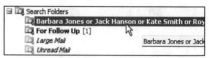

**Figure 4.29** Selecting the Search Folder you want to delete.

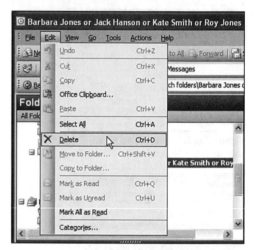

**Figure 4.30** Choosing Edit > Delete to delete the Search Folder.

**Figure 4.31** The dialog box prompting you to confirm Search Folder deletion.

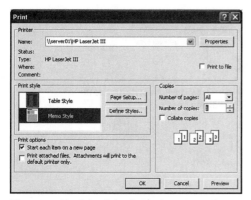

**Figure 4.32** The Print dialog box as it appears when the Messages view (a table view) of the Inbox folder is active.

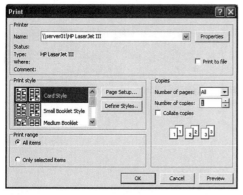

**Figure 4.33** The Print dialog box as it appears when the Address Cards view of the Contacts folder is active.

# Other Outlook Folder Operations

In the following sections, you'll learn how to print an entire Outlook folder—or one or more individual items within a folder. You'll also learn how to change an Outlook folder's properties.

### To print an Outlook folder or folder items:

1. Open the Outlook folder you want to print or the folder containing the items you want to print.

2. Switch to the view that displays the items the way you want to print them.

   Even if you're printing just a single item (rather than a whole folder), the current view affects the print styles that will be available.

3. If you want to print one or more individual items (rather than the entire folder), select them now.

4. Choose File > Print or press Ctrl+P to open the Print dialog box. **Figure 4.32** illustrates a Print dialog box for an email message, and a Calendar Item Print dialog box is displayed in **Figure 4.33**.

*continues on next page*

OTHER OUTLOOK FOLDER OPERATIONS

**5.** Choose the style you want for the printed output by selecting it in the Print Style list of the Print dialog box (**Figure 4.34**). The available styles depend upon the type of Outlook item selected:

▲ If a table view is active, you can select the Table Style, which prints the list of items in the folder, just as they appear in the Outlook window. Or, you can select the Memo Style, which prints the full contents of the individual item or items that you selected in step 2. (The Memo Style won't be available if you didn't select one or more items.)

▲ If another type of view is active, you'll probably have a wider choice of print styles. For example, with the Address Cards view of the Calendar folder, you can select the Card Style, Small Booklet Style, Medium Booklet Style, or Phone Directory Style.

**6.** In the Copies area of the Print dialog box (**Figure 4.35**), specify the pages to be printed, the number of copies, and whether the pages are to be collated. Or, just accept the defaults.

**7.** If necessary, in the Printer area of the Print dialog box (**Figure 4.36**), select a different printer in the Name list box or change the printer settings by clicking the Properties button.

**8.** In the area below the Print Style list, labeled Print Range or Print Options, select the options you want. The available options depend on the print style that's currently selected.

**Figure 4.34** The Print Style area of the Print dialog box.

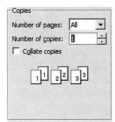

**Figure 4.35** The Copies area of the Print dialog box.

**Figure 4.36** The Printer area of the Print dialog box.

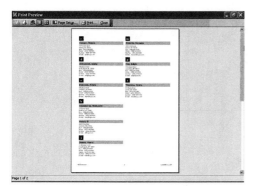

**Figure 4.37** The Print Preview window, showing the printed appearance of the Address Cards view of the Calendar folder (with the Card Style print style).

**9.** If you want to see what the printed output will look like before you start using paper, click the Preview button. Outlook will display the printed appearance of each page in the Print Preview window (**Figure 4.37**), reflecting the current settings in the Print dialog box. When you're ready to print—or to adjust print settings—click the Print button on the toolbar at the top of the window to return to the Print dialog box.

**10.** Click the OK button in the Print dialog box to start printing.

## ✔ Tips

- I recommend that you don't print in the Outlook window by clicking the Print button on the Standard toolbar, because the results are unpredictable.

  Sometimes Outlook opens the Print dialog box so you can adjust settings and preview the output, but other times it immediately prints.

- In the Print dialog box, you can click the Page Setup button to customize the currently selected print style. You can adjust the format, paper size, headers and footers, and other features of the printed output.

- In the Print dialog box, you can click the Define Styles button to modify any of the available print styles or to create new custom print styles.

- If you've opened an item in a form, you can print just that item by choosing File > Print in the form, which opens the Print dialog box. Or, you can just click the Print button on the form's Standard toolbar to immediately print the item using the default settings, without opening the Print dialog box. When you print an item in a form, Outlook uses the Memo Style print style.

**OTHER OUTLOOK FOLDER OPERATIONS**

## To change a folder's properties:

1. Open the folder whose properties you want to change.

2. Choose File > Folder > Properties For "Folder," where Folder is the name of the currently opened folder.

   Outlook will open the Folder Properties dialog box (**Figure 4.38**).

3. Change properties in the tabs of the Properties dialog box as desired:

   ▲ In the General tab, you can modify the folder's name (but only for a folder you have created) or the folder's description. You can also click the Folder Size button to determine the size of the folder and any subfolders it contains locally or on the Exchange Server (**Figure 4.39**).

   ▲ The Home Page tab lets you assign a home page to the folder. See the section "Attaching a Home Page to an Outlook Folder" in Chapter 14.

   ▲ The AutoArchive tab lets you define settings for automatically archiving the folder. This tab is explained in the section "To archive automatically" in Chapter 3. (This tab isn't included in the Properties dialog box for a contact-item folder because you can't automatically archive this folder type.)

   ▲ The Properties dialog box for a contact-item folder also includes Outlook Address Book and Activities tabs (the purpose of the Outlook Address Book tab is described in "Setting Up and Modifying the Email Configuration" in Appendix A, "Configuring Outlook").

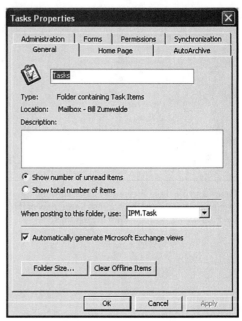

**Figure 4.38** The Properties dialog box for the Tasks folder.

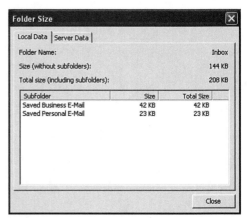

**Figure 4.39** The information displayed when you click Folder Size in the General tab of the Properties dialog box.

▲ If you're using Outlook with Exchange Server, the Properties tab might include four additional tabs: Administration, Forms, Permissions, and Synchronization. The Permissions tab was explained in the section "Sharing Outlook Folders over a Network," earlier in the chapter. The others are advanced features that aren't covered in this book.

## ✔ Tip

■ You can open the Properties dialog box for any folder, without first opening that folder, by right-clicking the folder in the permanently displayed Folder List and then choosing Properties from the pop-up menu.

**OTHER OUTLOOK FOLDER OPERATIONS**

# USING
# OUTLOOK TODAY

Outlook Today is a special folder view that displays a Web-style page which lets you quickly view current information in several commonly used Outlook folders:

- **Calendar**. Outlook Today displays your appointments, meetings, and all-day events for the next five days.

- **Tasks**. Outlook Today displays a list of all your tasks.

- **Messages**. Outlook Today shows the number of unread messages in your Inbox and the total numbers of messages in your Drafts and Outbox folders.

You can use Outlook Today to open any folder or item that it displays, as well as to mark tasks as completed.

In this chapter, you'll learn how to

- Work with the Outlook Today folder

- Customize Outlook Today

## ✔ Tip

- The Outlook Today techniques in the first main section of this chapter apply to the default Outlook Today setup. You should read through the entire chapter before you customize Outlook Today.

# Working with Outlook Today

**Figure 5.1** shows Outlook with the Outlook Today page opened. The page consists of three main columns, one for each type of information it displays.

Outlook Today is at the top of the hierarchy of folders in your Personal Folders file (**Figure 5.2**), or—if you're using Exchange Server—in your mailbox (**Figure 5.3**). It's the folder that contains all your other folders. The top branch of the folder list isn't labeled Outlook Today—it generally is named either Personal Folders (for a PST) or Mailbox (for an Exchange Server account).

## ✔ Tip

■ Outlook Today is a special Outlook folder that has been assigned a home page. You don't store items in Outlook Today. Rather, you work with its home page, which contains the elements that are described in this chapter. So, think of Outlook Today as a Web view of your most frequently used Outlook folders.

**Figure 5.2** Hierarchy of folders in your Personal Folders (.PST) file.

**Figure 5.3** Hierarchy of folders in your mailbox (Exchange Server).

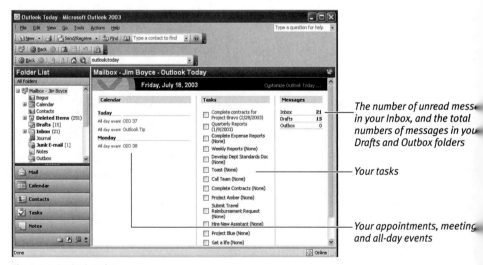

*The number of unread mess[...] in your Inbox, and the total numbers of messages in you[...] Drafts and Outbox folders*

*Your tasks*

*Your appointments, meeting[...] and all-day events*

**Figure 5.1** Outlook Today.

**Figure 5.4** The Outlook Today shortcut.

**Figure 5.5** Opening Outlook Today from the Navigation pane.

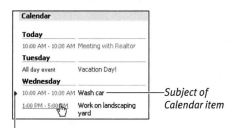

*Subject of Calendar item*

*Red triangle marks your first appointment*

**Figure 5.6** Working with your Calendar items.

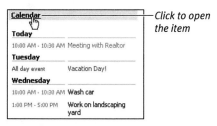

*Click to open the item*

**Figure 5.7** Opening your Wednesday afternoon appointment.

## To open Outlook Today:

◆ Click the Outlook Today shortcut in the Advanced Outlook Toolbar (**Figure 5.4**).

*or*

Click the Personal Folders folder in the Navigation Pane (**Figure 5.5**), or click Mailbox in the Navigation pane.

## ✔ Tip

■ You can have Outlook automatically open the Outlook Today folder whenever you start the program. See "To customize Outlook Today," later in the chapter.

## To work with your Calendar items:

◆ Open any of the Calendar items that are displayed—an appointment, event, or meeting—by clicking on it. You can click on the date or the subject (**Figure 5.6**).

*or*

Open the Calendar folder by clicking on the gray Calendar header at the top of the column.

## ✔ Tip

■ When you point to an item or folder name in Outlook Today, the text is underlined and the mouse pointer turns into a hand, indicating that you can click to open the item or folder (**Figure 5.7**).

WORKING WITH OUTLOOK TODAY

## To work with your tasks:

1. To open the Tasks folder, click on the gray Tasks header at the top of the column.

2. To open a task, click on the task description. You can click on the subject or due date—not on the check box (**Figure 5.8**).

3. To mark a task as completed, click on the check box to its left. Outlook will check the box and draw a line through the task, marking it as completed (**Figure 5.9**).

## To work with your messages:

◆ Click a folder name to open the folder (**Figure 5.10**). You can open the Inbox by clicking Inbox or by clicking the gray Messages header at the top of the column.

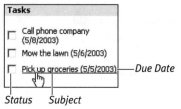

**Figure 5.8** Working with your tasks.

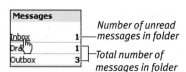

**Figure 5.9** A task that's been checked as completed.

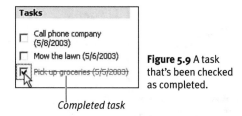

**Figure 5.10** Working with your messages.

WORKING WITH OUTLOOK TODAY

**Figure 5.11** Clicking the button that opens the Customize Outlook Today page.

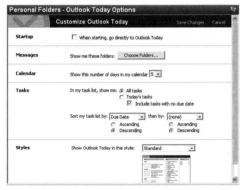

**Figure 5.12** The Customize Outlook Today page of the Outlook Today folder.

# Customizing Outlook Today

You can customize Outlook Today according to your preferences and work habits. Specifically, you can do the following:

◆ Have Outlook automatically open the Outlook Today folder whenever you start the program.

◆ Specify the mail-item folders that are listed in the Messages column of Outlook Today.

◆ Change the number of days of Calendar items that are displayed in Outlook Today.

◆ Choose which tasks are displayed and the way they're sorted.

◆ Modify the overall style of the Outlook Today page.

## To customize Outlook Today:

1. Open the Outlook Today folder and click the Customize Outlook Today button in the upper-right corner of the page (**Figure 5.11**).

   Outlook will open the Customize Outlook Today page of the Outlook Today folder (**Figure 5.12**).

*continues on next page*

**CUSTOMIZING OUTLOOK TODAY**

**2.** In the Customize Outlook Today page, select customization options as desired:

▲ To have Outlook automatically open Outlook Today each time you start the program, check When Starting, Go Directly to Outlook Today.

▲ To change the folders displayed in the Messages column, click the Choose Folders button, and in the Select Folder dialog box (**Figure 5.13**), check each folder you want to be displayed and then click the OK button.

▲ To change the number of days of Calendar items that are displayed in the Calendar column, select a number in the Show This Number of Days in My Calendar list box.

▲ To show only the current day's tasks, select the Today's Tasks option. If you want to display all of the days' tasks, check Include Tasks with No Due Date.

▲ To change the sorting order of tasks, select a primary sorting field in the Sort My Task List By list box, and select a secondary sorting field in the Then By list box. Under each list box, select either Ascending or Descending to specify the sorting order used with the field.

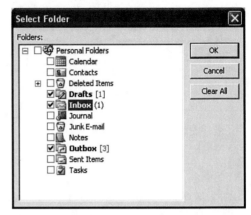

**Figure 5.13** The Select Folder dialog box.

*Preview image of style*

**Figure 5.14** Selecting a style.

**Figure 5.15** Outlook Today with the Summer style.

▲ To change the overall look of the Outlook Today folder, select a new style in the Show Outlook Today in This Style list box. The default style shown in Figure 5.1 is Standard. When you select a style, Outlook displays a preview image of that style below the list box (**Figure 5.14**). The Summer style is shown in **Figure 5.15**.

3. Click the Save Changes button in the upper-right corner to save the new settings you made, return to the main page of Outlook Today, and apply the changes.

   *or*

   Click the Cancel button to discard your settings and return to the main page of Outlook Today.

# USING THE INBOX TO MANAGE MESSAGES

**6**

You can use the Outlook Inbox folder—as well as the other mail-item folders (Drafts, Outbox, and Sent Items)—to receive, send, and manage email, and send fax messages. Here's how these folders are normally used:

◆ Incoming email messages are delivered to your Inbox by a mail account or by an email information service.

◆ While you are composing a message, before you send it, it's normally stored in the Drafts folder.

◆ When you send a message, it's temporarily stored in the Outbox folder until the next time Outlook connects to the mail server to process outgoing messages, thereby sending it to the recipient. Sometimes messages are transmitted immediately and are stored in your Outbox only briefly, because Outlook connects to your mail server right away to send the outgoing message.

◆ A copy of each message you send is normally stored in your Sent Items folder.

In this chapter, you'll learn how to:

◆ Receive email messages in your Inbox.

◆ Read email messages and open or save file attachments.

- Use Instant Messaging

- Send email messages

- Send fax messages

- Organize your messages with rules

- Block junk email

## ✔ Tips

- The instructions in this chapter assume that you've already set up your email and fax accounts or information services, as explained in Chapter 1, "Setting Up Outlook 2003," and Appendix A, "Configuring Outlook."

- The instructions also assume that you've opened your Inbox or another mail-item folder. (Otherwise, you won't find some of the commands mentioned.)

- The different ways to open folders are explained in "Opening an Outlook folder" in Chapter 2, "Getting Started Using Outlook.". Keep in mind that with the initial Outlook setup, the icons for the Inbox , Drafts, Outbox, and Sent Items folders are in the Folder List.

**Figure 6.1** Send/receive groups control how and when messages are sent.

# Receiving Email Messages

You can have Outlook automatically receive your email messages from one or more accounts at specified intervals, or you can manually receive them at any time. If you don't set up automatic receiving, then you'll have to receive manually.

The procedure for setting up automatic receiving depends upon whether an email account uses a full-time Internet connection or a dial-up connection. A full-time connection is one that provides access to the Internet at all times, usually through a company local area network (LAN) connected to your computer. A dial-up connection uses a modem in your computer and is typically made only when you are actually exchanging email or accessing an Internet site.

Outlook uses send/receive groups to logically manage mail accounts. Send/receive groups consist of one or more email accounts in any combination (**Figure 6.1**). This section explains how to use send/receive groups to process messages. See Chapter 12, "Using Advanced Features," to learn how to create, change, and manage send/receive groups.

## ✔ Tips

- The different types of connections are described in the section "To add a Mail Account with the Internet Connection Wizard" in Appendix A.

- When Outlook receives email messages, it might also transmit outgoing email messages from your Outbox, as described later in the chapter.

## To receive email messages automatically for all accounts:

1. Choose Tools > Options and click the Mail Setup tab in the Options dialog box.

2. Check the Send/Receive button to display the Send/Receive dialog box.

3. In the Send/Receive Groups dialog box, highlight the Group Name you want to configure. Check the box Schedule an Automatic Send/Receive Every "number" Minutes. Enter the desired interval in minutes at which you want Outlook to automatically receive your email messages. Then, click Close.

4. If one or more of your email accounts uses a dial-up connection, check the Automatically Dial During a Background Send/Receive option (**Figure 6.2**) in the Mail Setup tab. (If you don't check this option, a dial-up account will be skipped when Outlook automatically receives email.)

5. Click the OK button.

   Outlook will then begin receiving your email messages at the interval you specified (**Figure 6.3**), automatically dialing your modem for any account that uses dial-up access. It will place any messages you receive in your Inbox folder.

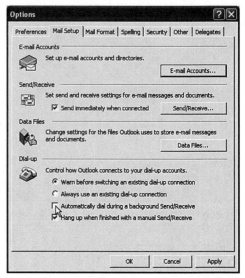

**Figure 6.2** Selecting options on the Mail Setup tab of the Options dialog box to have Outlook automatically receive your email messages (via a full-time or dial-up account).

**Figure 6.3** The dialog box that Outlook displays when it's receiving and sending email.

RECEIVING EMAIL MESSAGES

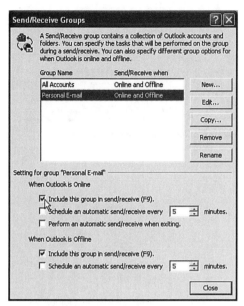

Figure 6.4 The Send/Receive Groups dialog box.

Figure 6.5 The Offline icon on the Status bar indicating that you're working online or offline.

## ✔ Tips

■ Outlook will automatically receive email only from accounts that have the Include This Account When Receiving Mail or Synchronizing option checked. To access this option, choose Tools > Options, click the Mail Setup tab and click Send/Receive. In the Send/Receive Groups dialog box, select the group name and check the box Include This Group in Send/Receive (F9). Then click Close (**Figure 6.4**). (This option is enabled by default.)

■ If you do not configure an email account to store your password, Outlook will prompt for the password each time it attempts an automatic send/receive. To fully automate the process, direct Outlook to save your password for the account when prompted.

■ If you are working offline, Outlook will not automatically receive email from an account with full-time Internet access. It will, however, continue to automatically dial up and receive email from an account with dial-up access. To switch between working online and working offline, choose File > Work Offline. When you're working offline, an Offline icon appears at the right end of the status bar and the right end of the System Tray (**Figure 6.5**).

■ If you're working offline and manually receive email messages (as described next), Outlook switches you back to working online temporarily for the Send/Receive process, and then switches back to working offline.

■ You can also open the Send/Receive Groups dialog box by choosing Tools > Send/Receive > Send/Receive Settings > Define Send/Receive Groups. You can also press Ctrl+Alt+S to open the dialog box.

## To receive email messages manually:

◆ To receive email from all your enabled email accounts, click the Send/Receive button on the Standard toolbar, or choose Tools > Send/Receive > Send/Receive All, or press F9.

*or*

To receive email from a specific account (whether or not it's enabled), choose Tools > Send/Receive and then choose the name of the Send/Receive group from the submenu (**Figure 6.6**).

Outlook will then connect with the email account or accounts, and it will place any messages you receive in your Inbox folder.

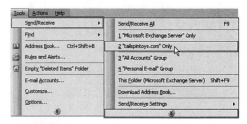

**Figure 6.6** Receiving messages from just the tailspintoys.com account.

*A file attachment*

*A message flagged for follow-up*

*A message marked as High Importance*

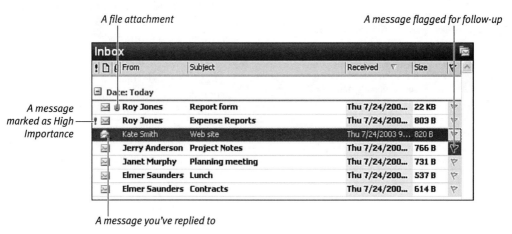

*A message you've replied to*

**Figure 6.7** Email messages listed in the Inbox.

*The selected message*   *The Reading pane*

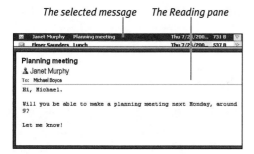

**Figure 6.8** Reading a message in the Reading pane.

*Message header*

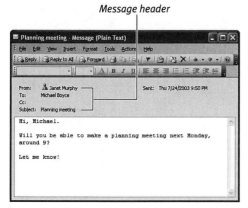

**Figure 6.9** Reading a message in the Message form.

# Reading Email Messages

Outlook will deliver your incoming email messages from all email accounts to your Inbox (**Figure 6.7**). You can read any email message it contains either by using the Reading pane or by opening the message in a Message form.

## To read an email message:

1. Open the Inbox folder and click the email message to select it.

2. If the Reading pane isn't currently displayed, click the Reading Pane button on the Advanced toolbar or choose View > Reading Pane and select either Right or Bottom depending on your preference. You can then view the selected message in this pane, without having to open it (**Figure 6. 8**).

   *or*

   Double-click the message, or use one of the other methods for opening an item described in "To open an item" in Chapter 3. The message will be displayed in a Message form (**Figure 6.9**).

## ✔ Tips

- In the Outlook window, an unread message is marked with bold formatting (**Figure 6.10**). You can change the marking of a message by selecting it and choosing Edit > Mark As Read or Edit > Mark As Unread, or you can choose Edit > Mark All As Read to remove the bold marking from all messages in the folder.

- If you've chosen Word as your email editor, a message will be opened in Word rather than in the Outlook Message form (unless the message is in HTML format). See "Email editors and formats," later in the chapter.

- If you want to flag a message for special attention, open the message and click the Flag For Follow Up button on the form's toolbar. Then define the flag in the Flag For Follow Up dialog box (**Figure 6.11**).

- You can hide or show the message header in the Message form (**Figure 6.12**) by choosing View > Message Header. When you hide the header, only the From and Sent fields are shown.

- You can set other options for a message by opening the message in a form and choosing View > Options to open the Message Options dialog box (**Figure 6.13**). This dialog box also lets you view the message's Internet headers, which show technical information on the sending and routing of the message. Often, you can determine the true sender of a message by viewing the header; for example, determining if a message is from someone you know or from a spammer (someone who sends unsolicited junk mail).

**Figure 6.10** Unread messages appear in bold.

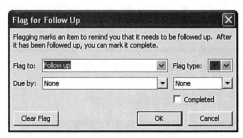

**Figure 6.11** The Flag For Follow Up dialog box.

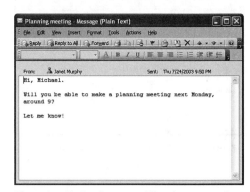

**Figure 6.12** The header removed from the message form.

**Figure 6.13** The Message Options dialog box for an incoming message in the Inbox.

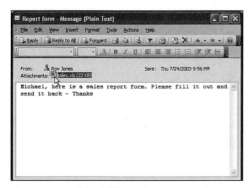

**Figure 6.14** Double-clicking a file attachment icon to open the file.

*Right-click here to open the menu*

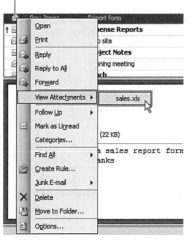

**Figure 6.15** Opening a file attachment by using the drop-down menu.

**Figure 6.16** Choosing to open a file attachment in the Opening Mail Attachment dialog box.

## To open a file attachment included in an email message:

1. View the message in the Reading pane or open it in a form, and double-click the icon for the file attachment (**Figure 6.14**).

   *or*

   In the Inbox, right-click on the message, choose View Attachments, and choose the name of the attachment from the submenu (**Figure 6.15**).

2. If Outlook displays the Opening Mail Attachment dialog box (**Figure 6.16**), select Open and click the OK button.

The file attachment will then be opened in the appropriate program. For example, if you have Microsoft Word installed, a file attachment with the .doc extension will be opened in Word.

## ✔ Tips

- Don't open a file attachment in a message from an unknown source! Certain types of attachments can contain viruses, and opening an attachment might allow a virus to harm your computer.

- Outlook blocks certain types of attachments, preventing you from opening them. Outlook refers to these as Level 1 Attachments. You can find a list of these attachment types by opening Help and opening the following Help document from the Table of Contents: Security and Privacy\Security\Attachment file types blocked by Outlook. If you need access to a particular blocked attachment, export the message to Outlook Express and read it there, or forward it to a Web-based email account such as Hotmail, where you will be able to download the attachment.

*continues on next page*

- Exchange Server supports Level 2 attachments, which Outlook does not allow you to open directly, but which you can save to disk from Outlook in order to open. An Exchange Server administrator must configure Level 2 attachments on the Exchange Server—you cannot control these attachment types from Outlook. If you remove attachment types from the Level 1 list (see previous tips), Outlook treats them as Level 2 attachments.

### To save a file attachment in a disk file:

1. In the Outlook window, select the message that has the attachment you want to save.

2. Choose File > Save Attachments, and then from the submenu choose the name of the individual attachment you want to save (**Figure 6.17**), or choose All Attachments to save all in one step.

3. In the Save Attachment dialog box (**Figure 6.18**), select the disk location where you want to save the file.

   If you wish, you can change the name of the file by typing a new name in the File Name text box.

4. Click the Save button.

**Figure 6.17** Saving the Chapter 2.doc file attachment.

**Figure 6.18** Selecting a disk location for a file attachment in the Save Attachment dialog box.

**Figure 6.19** The Save All Attachments dialog box.

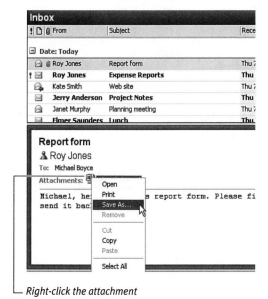

Right-click the attachment

**Figure 6.20** Saving an attachment from a pop-up menu.

## ✔ Tips

■ If a message has more than one file attachment, you can save several attachments at once by choosing File > Save Attachments > All Attachments in step 2 and then selecting the specific attachments you want to save in the Save All Attachments dialog box (**Figure 6.19**).

■ If a message is open in a form, you can save one or more attachments by choosing File > Save Attachments.

■ If a message is displayed in the Reading pane or opened in a form, you can save a single file attachment by right-clicking the attachment's icon and choosing Save As from the pop-up menu (**Figure 6.20**).

# Sending Email Messages

Sending email normally consists of the following two main steps:

1. Create the email message. You create an email message in the Message form. You can either create a new message or reply to or forward a message that you've received.

   When you click the Send button in the form, the message is initially stored in your Outbox folder. In the following two cases, however, a message is stored in your Outbox for only a few seconds, making it appear as if the message never reached your Outbox:

   ▲ If the Send Immediately When Connected option is checked, and if a message is sent via a full-time connection or a dial-up connection that's already connected, the message will be sent immediately. You access this option by choosing Tools > Options, and clicking the Mail Setup tab (**Figure 6.21**).

   ▲ With an Exchange Server account working in online mode, messages are delivered immediately to the server, remaining in the Outbox only briefly.

2. Transmit your email messages from the Outbox to their recipients.

Outlook makes a copy of each transmitted message in your Sent Items folder, provided that the Save Copies of Messages in Sent Items Folder option is checked. You access this option by choosing Tools > Options and clicking the E-mail Options button on the Preferences tab (**Figure 6.22**).

The instructions for completing these two steps are given in the following sections.

*Check this option*

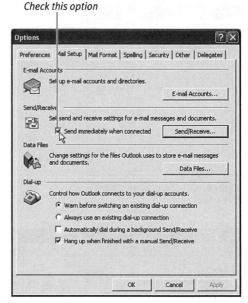

**Figure 6.21** Having Outlook immediately transmit messages as soon as you click the Send button in the Message form.

*Check this option*

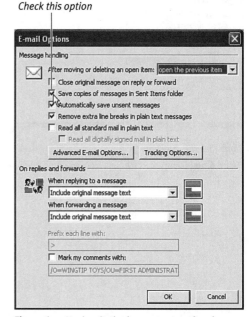

**Figure 6.22** Having Outlook save a copy of each transmitted message in your Sent Items folder.

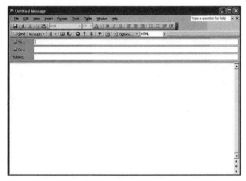

**Figure 6.23** A blank Message form for creating a new outgoing email message.

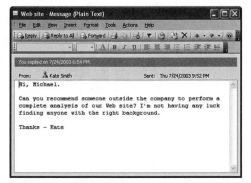

**Figure 6.24** The Message form that is opened when you reply to an incoming email message.

## To create a new email message:

1. Open a mail-item folder such as Inbox and click the New button on the Standard toolbar, or choose Actions > New > Mail Message, or press Ctrl+N.

   *or*

   Press Ctrl+Shift+M. (Any folder can be open.)

   Outlook will open an empty Message form (**Figure 6.23**).

2. Complete the Message form and send the message, as explained in "To complete the Message form," later in the chapter.

## To reply to or forward an email message:

1. Open the folder containing the incoming message you want to reply to, or forward and select the message.

   *or*

   Open the incoming message in the Message form.

2. Click one of the following buttons on the Standard toolbar in the Outlook window or in the form:

   ▲ **Reply**. The new message will be addressed to the sender of the incoming message, and its subject will contain the subject from the incoming message, prefaced with RE: (**Figure 6.24**).

   ▲ **Reply to All**. The new message will be addressed to the sender of the incoming message, and copies of the message will be sent to everyone who originally received a copy of the incoming message (that is, their addresses will be inserted in the Cc field, which you'll learn about later). The new message's subject will contain the subject from the incoming message, prefaced with RE:.

*continues on next page*

**SENDING EMAIL MESSAGES**

▲ **Forward**. The new message's subject will contain the subject from the incoming message, prefaced with FW: (**Figure 6.25**).

Whichever button you click, the new message body (the large text box) will contain the header and text from the incoming message.

3. Complete the Message form and send the message, as explained in "To complete the Message form," below. If you're replying to a message, type your reply above the original text. If you're forwarding a message, you can type a comment or explanation, if you wish, above the original text.

## ✔ Tip

■ You can modify the way Outlook formats the original text in a reply or in a forwarded message by choosing Tools > Options, clicking the E-mail Options button on the Preferences tab, and selecting options in the On Replies and Forwards area of the E-mail Options dialog box (**Figure 6.26**).

## To complete the Message form:

1. Enter the message recipient or recipients in the To text box. For details on how to do this, see "To address a message" later in the chapter.

   **Figures 6.23** through **6.25** show several Message forms, before new information has been entered.

2. If you want to send a copy of the message to one or more other people, enter them in the Cc text box. For details on how to do this, see "To address a message" later in the chapter.

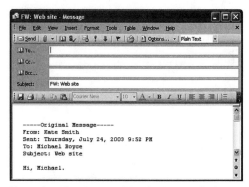

**Figure 6.25** The Message form that is opened when you forward an incoming email message.

*Select options here to modify the way Outlook formats the original text it inserts in replies or forwarded messages*

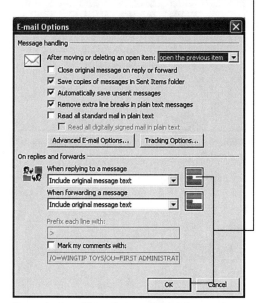

**Figure 6.26** Modifying the way Outlook formats the original text in replies and forwarded messages.

**Figure 6.27** Inserting a file into an email message.

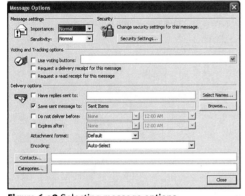

**Figure 6.28** Selecting message options.

**3.** Type a message subject in the Subject text box. The recipient will see this text in his or her email program before opening the message.

**4.** Type the body of the message in the large text box. See the section "Editing Items" in Chapter 3 for information on entering, editing, and formatting the text.

**5.** If you want to attach a file to the message, click the Insert File button on the form's Standard toolbar, or choose Insert > File. Then, in the Insert File dialog box, select the file and click the Insert button (**Figure 6.27**).

**6.** To select options for the message, click the Options button on the Standard toolbar, or choose View > Options. Then select the desired options in the Message Options dialog box (**Figure 6.28**) and click the Close button.

**Figure 6.29** shows a completed Message form.

*continues on next page*

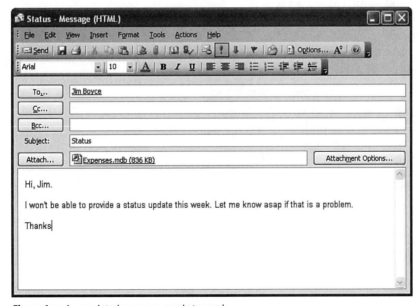

**Figure 6.29** A completed message, ready to send.

**SENDING EMAIL MESSAGES**

**7.** Click the Send button on the form's Standard toolbar.

At this point, Outlook will normally place the message in your Outbox, and you'll need to transmit it to the recipient, as explained later in the chapter. (See the exceptions that were discussed at the beginning of "Sending Email Messages," earlier in the chapter.)

## ✔ Tips

■ If you have more than one email account, you can specify the account that will be used to send the message by clicking the Accounts button adjacent to the Send button on the form's Standard toolbar and choosing the name of the account from the drop-down menu (**Figure 6.30**). (If you just click the Send button, the message will be sent using your default email account.) This applies to new messages as well as replies and forwards.

■ The header for a message in your Outbox that's ready to transmit is formatted in italics (**Figure 6.31**). If you reopen the message before it's transmitted, be sure to click the Send button again. Otherwise, the message won't be transmitted (as indicated by its non-italic formatting).

■ The forms and dialog boxes shown in this section are those displayed when you're using Word as your email editor. They are somewhat different if you use Outlook email editor and the Microsoft Outlook Rich Text format or select another email format. See "To change your email editor or format," later in the chapter.

*Select an account*

**Figure 6.30** Choosing a specific account for sending a message.

**Figure 6.31** A message in the Outbox that's ready to transmit.

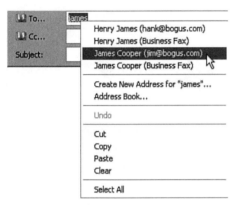

**Figure 6.32** Two email addresses typed directly in the To text box.

**Figure 6.33** After I typed **Fred** in the To text box, Outlook found a unique matching name in my Contacts folder. It then completed and underlined the name.

**Figure 6.34** After I typed **james** in the To text box, Outlook found two matching contacts and underlined the name with a red wavy line. I right-clicked the name and chose the recipient I wanted, James Cooper, from the pop-up menu.

**Figure 6.35** The result of choosing the name from the pop-up menu shown in **Figure 6.34**.

## To address a message:

◆ In the Message form, type the recipient's exact Internet email address directly in the To or Cc text box. If you want to enter several addresses in a single text box, separate them with semicolons (**Figure 6.32**).

*or*

If the recipient's email address is in your Contacts folder (or if you want to search for it using an Internet directory service), type part or all of the person's name as it appears in Contacts in the To or Cc text box. When you exit the field, Outlook automatically looks for the name in Contacts. Then:

▲ If Outlook finds a unique match, it completes the name (if necessary) and underlines it with a solid black line to indicate that the name has been verified (**Figure 6.33**). Outlook will use the email address (if any) associated with the contact to address your message.

▲ If Outlook finds more than one contact matching the name you typed, it underlines the name with a wavy red line. Right-click the name and choose the person you want from the pop-up menu (**Figures 6.34** and **6.35**).

▲ If Outlook finds more than one contact matching the name you typed, but you previously typed the same name and chose a name from the pop-up menu, it displays your previous choice and underlines it with a dashed green line. You can right-click the name and choose another name if you want.

▲ If Outlook doesn't find a match, it leaves the name as is, and you'll have to type another name or use one of the other addressing methods.

*continues on next page*

*or*

Click the To or Cc button in the message header, or click the Address Book button on the form's Standard toolbar, or press Ctrl+Shift+B. Outlook will open the Select Names dialog box (**Figure 6.36**), which lets you transfer names to the To, Cc, and Bcc message fields from your Contacts folder or from an Internet directory service. Outlook will use the email address associated with each name you transfer. You work with this dialog box as follows:

▲ Select a name in the list of contacts and then click the To, Cc, or Bcc button to copy the name to the To, Cc, or Bcc field in your message.

▲ To quickly locate a name in a long list of contacts, type the start of the name in the Type Name or Select from List text box at the top of the dialog box.

▲ If you have more than one contact-item folder, you can view the items in a particular one by selecting it in the list box.

▲ To look up an email address using an Internet directory service, select the directory service in the Show Names From The list box. Click the Advanced button and select Find from the menu. In the Find dialog box (**Figure 6.37**), type the person's name in the Display Name text box, and click the OK button. If matches are found, they are displayed at the bottom of the dialog box, and you can select the name you want and click the To, Cc, or Bcc button to copy the name and address to the corresponding field in your message.

*Select an alternative contact-item folder or address list here*

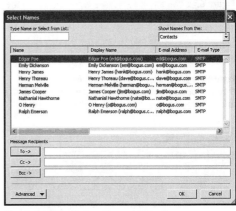

**Figure 6.36** The Select Names dialog box.

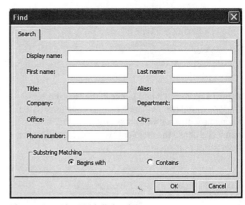

**Figure 6.37** The Find dialog box.

**Figure 6.38** Click to show the Bcc field.

**Figure 6.39** Show the Bcc field for only the current message.

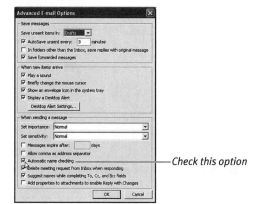

*Check this option*

**Figure 6.40** Turning on automatic name checking.

*Type a name to locate in the address book*

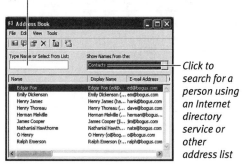

*Click to search for a person using an Internet directory service or other address list*

**Figure 6.41** The Address Book dialog box.

## ✔ Tips

- The Find box in directory services (**Figure 6.37**) allows searching with more fields than just a name. Use the Contains and Begins With options to specify how the information you enter is matched by Outlook against the LDAP server.

- If you enter an address in the Bcc message field, a copy of the message will be sent to that address, but other message recipients won't see the address. (An address that's entered in the Cc field is generally revealed to all message recipients.) To display a text box for the Bcc field with Outlook as your email editor (**Figure 6.38**), choose View > Bcc Field. To display the Bcc field with Word as your email editor (**Figure 6.39**), choose the down arrow on the right of the Options button and choose Bcc from the menu.

- To have Outlook automatically check names in the To, Cc, and Bcc fields, the Automatic Name Checking option must be checked. You access this option by choosing Tools > Options, clicking the E-mail Options button on the Preferences tab, and then clicking the Advanced E-mail Options button (**Figure 6.40**).

- If automatic name checking is turned off, you can check names manually by clicking the Check Names button on the form's Standard toolbar.

- In the main Outlook window, you can open the Address Book dialog box (**Figure 6.41**) by choosing Tools > Address Book or pressing Ctrl+Shift+B. Like the Select Names dialog box, it lets you access the items in your Contacts folder or search for people using any of your address lists

*continues on next page*

**SENDING EMAIL MESSAGES**

- Rather than selecting an individual name from your Contacts folder, you can select a distribution list, which sends the message to an entire group of people. For information on defining distribution lists, see "Creating Contact Items" in Chapter 8, "Using the Contacts Folder."

- If you have more than one email information service, the particular service that will be used to transmit the message depends upon which account is set as the default account (**Figure 6.42**). To change the default account, highlight the desired account and select Set as Default (**Figure 6.43**). That account is then displayed at the top of the order list.

  *or*

  Choose Move Up or Move Down to set the order of processing for the accounts. The account at the top automatically becomes the Default account.

- To send a message from a specific service account, click on the Accounts button and choose the account desired (**Figure 6.44**). The email item will then be sent from that account.

- Rather than selecting an individual address from your Contacts address list, you can select a distribution list, which sends the message to an entire group of people. For information on defining distribution lists in the Contacts folder, see "Creating Contact Items" in Chapter 8.

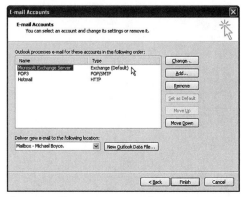

**Figure 6.42** The top account sends outgoing messages by default.

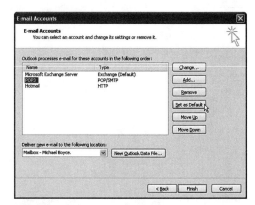

**Figure 6.43** Setting a different default mail account.

**Figure 6.44** Selecting the outgoing account while composing the message.

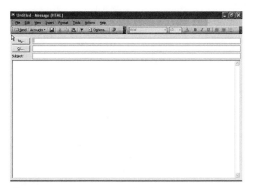

**Figure 6.45** Using the Outlook editor to compose a message.

# Email Editors and Formats

You can use either of the following two editors to read or send email messages:

◆ The built-in **Outlook editor**, which is used in the standard Message form. The Outlook editor is fast and probably has all the features you need (**Figure 6.45**).

◆ The figures presented so far in this chapter have shown the **Word editor** and the advanced Message form. Although it's slower starting, it provides many sophisticated features not available in the Outlook editor—for example, alternative document views; formatting styles; automatic insertion, correction, and formatting of text; and checking of spelling as you type.

Whichever editor you employ, you can use any of the following basic formats for the new email messages you create:

◆ **Plain text** doesn't let you format text or add graphics, but it can be read by virtually any recipient. If you use this format, the formatting and graphics commands in the Message form are disabled. Deceptively, in Word you can use the formatting or graphics commands, but formatting and graphics are removed when you save or send the message.

◆ **Rich Text** lets you format text—change fonts, italicize, indent paragraphs, and so on—and insert graphics. Many recipients, however, won't be able to view the formatting. With this format, you can use the formatting commands described in the section "Formatting Text" in Chapter 3.

*continues on next page*

EMAIL EDITORS AND FORMATS

◆ **HTML** (hypertext markup language, the format used for Web pages), lets you format text, insert pictures, assign styles to text (such as Heading 1 or Bulleted List), apply a background picture or color to the message, insert horizontal dividing lines, and get a head start in creating attractive messages by using predesigned stationery. Many recipients, however, won't be able to view these HTML features. **Figure 6.46** shows some of the additional commands available in the Message form with the HTML format.

## ✔ Tips

- When you reply to or forward an email message, Outlook matches the format of the incoming message.

- If a recipient's email service or program doesn't transmit or display Rich Text or HTML, a plain text version of the message will generally be displayed. But you can avoid wasted effort by not sending formatted or graphical messages to such users.

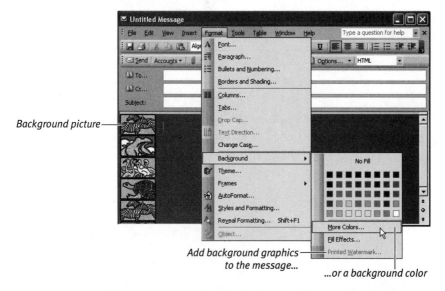

Background picture

Add background graphics to the message...

...or a background color

**Figure 6.46** Commands available in the Message form only when you use the HTML format. Not shown are the Insert menu commands for inserting a horizontal line, a picture, or a hyperlink.

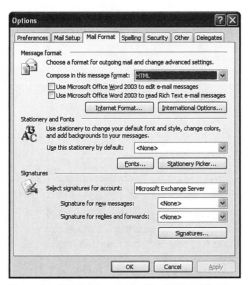

**Figure 6.47** The Mail Format tab of the Options dialog box.

**Figure 6.48** The Stationery picker dialog box.

## To change your email editor or format:

1. Choose Tools > Options and open the Mail Format tab in the Options dialog box (**Figure 6.47**).

2. Select options as desired:
   - ▲ Choose the email format you wish to use in the Compose in This Message Format list box.
   - ▲ If you want to use Word as your email editor, check Use Microsoft Word to Edit E-Mail Messages. In this case, *none of the options described in the remainder of this list will be available.* You'll have to select the desired options within Word itself.
   - ▲ To select the default fonts used in your messages, click the Fonts button and select options in the Fonts dialog box.
   - ▲ If you selected the HTML format, you can choose default stationery to be used for your new messages in the Use This Stationery by Default list box. Or you can click the Stationery Picker button to preview each type of stationery in the Stationery Picker dialog box (**Figure 6.48**) and select the one you want. Using stationery to create a message adds a background picture and initial text to give you a head start in creating an attractive message for a particular purpose (such as a party invitation, formal announcement, or holiday card).

*continues on next page*

EMAIL EDITORS AND FORMATS

▲ You can have Outlook automatically insert a signature at the end of the email messages you create for each account. Select the account desired from the Select the Signatures to Use with the Following Account list box (**Figure 6.49**). Choose the signature from the Signature for New Messages and/or Signature for Replies and Forwards list box. A signature is a block of text that usually contains your name, profession, address, Web page, or other information. If you haven't yet created a signature, you'll need to click the Signatures button and then click the New button in the Create Signature dialog box (**Figure 6.50**) to compose a signature.

3. Click the OK button.

## ✔ Tips

■ You can create a new message using any email format, overriding the default, by choosing Actions > New Mail Message Using and then choosing a format on the submenu (**Figure 6.51**).

■ If you're using the Outlook editor by default, you can create a single message in Word—using the current default email format—by choosing Actions > New Mail Message Using > Microsoft Word (Format), where Format is the name of the current default email format (Plain Text, Rich Text, or HTML).

◆ If the recipient's email program does not support or accept HTML messages, the background does not appear in the message but (depending on the program) will be attached to the message as a file.

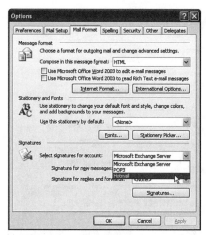

**Figure 6.49** Selecting an account to assign a signature.

**Figure 6.50** The Create Signature dialog box lets you view, edit, or create a signature.

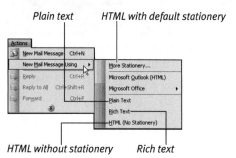

**Figure 6.51** Creating a new email message with a specific format, overriding the default format.

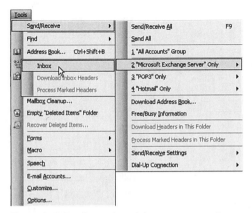

**Figure 6.52** Sending and receiving messages using a specific email account.

## To transmit messages from your Outbox:

◆ To transmit all messages in your Outbox, without receiving email, choose Tools > Send/Receive > Send All.

◆ To transmit all messages in your Outbox and to receive email from all enabled accounts or email information services, click the Send/Receive button on the Standard toolbar, or choose Tools > Send/Receive > Send/Receive All, or press F9. (For instructions on enabling specific accounts or information services for receiving email, see the earlier section "To receive email messages manually."

◆ To transmit only messages that are to be sent using a particular account or information service and to receive messages from that account or information service only, choose Tools > Send/Receive and then choose the account or information service name from the submenu (**Figure 6.52**). Outlook will transmit each message using the appropriate mail account or information service.

## ✔ Tips

■ If you want to resend a message— perhaps as a friendly reminder if the recipient hasn't yet replied—open the message (it will normally be stored in your Sent Items folder) and in the form choose Actions > Resend This Message.

■ You can send a fax message using a fax modem. To send an outgoing fax from Outlook, you must add the Fax Transport service to your profile (choose Tools > E-mail Accounts, click Add a New Email Account, Next, Additional Server Types) or use a third-party fax service. You can also print a document to the Fax Printer, which Windows adds automatically when you add a fax modem. However, faxing is not covered in this book.

# Organizing Your Messages with Rules

You can organize your email messages using the general techniques presented in Chapters 3 and 4. For example, those chapters show how you can create new folders for storing messages and how you can copy or move messages from one folder to another.

Chapter 3 (the section "Using the Organize Page") explained in general how to use the Organize Page to organize your Outlook items. In a mail-item folder, the Organize Page (**Figure 6.53**) provides several unique features for organizing and managing messages:

◆ You can have Outlook move a message to a specified folder.

◆ You can have Outlook color-code messages from or to a particular person. The messages will be displayed in your Inbox using the color you specify.

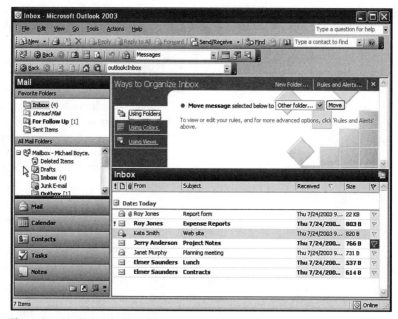

**Figure 6.53** Displaying the Organize Page in the Inbox folder.

## ✔ Tips

■ When you're done using the Organize Page, you can remove it by clicking the Close Organize button in the upper-right corner of the page.

■ The Rules Wizard provides much greater flexibility for creating rules than the Organize Page, but the Organize Page is generally easier for novices to use to create rules. See the section, "Using the Rules Wizard to have Outlook sort adult-content email," later in this chapter to learn more about the Rules Wizard.

■ To quickly create a rule from an existing message, right-click the message and choose Create Rule. Outlook displays a Create Rule dialog box in which you specify the conditions for the rule and the action you want the rule to take. This method provides a limited number of conditions and actions, but is great for quickly creating rules to move or notify you about messages that fit the specified conditions.

**ORGANIZING YOUR MESSAGES WITH RULES**

## To move a message:

1. In a mail-item folder, select a message you want Outlook to move.

2. Choose Tools > Organize to open the Organize Page.

3. Click Using Folders to display the folder options (**Figure 6.54**).

4. Select a message and click Move (**Figure 6.55**).

## To have Outlook color-code messages for a particular person:

1. In a mail-item folder, select a message from or to the person whose messages you want Outlook to color-code.

   You must open a mail-item folder, but selecting a message is optional, because you can later type the name.

2. Choose Tools > Organize to open the Organize Page.

3. Click Using Colors to display the color-coding options (**Figure 6.56**).

4. Use the Color Messages fields to describe the color-coding you want Outlook to perform (**Figure 6.56**).

**Figure 6.54** The folder options on the Organize Page.

*Select the destination folder*    *Click Move*

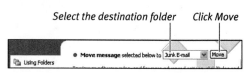

**Figure 6.55** Moving a message.

**Figure 6.56** The color-coding options on the Organize Page.

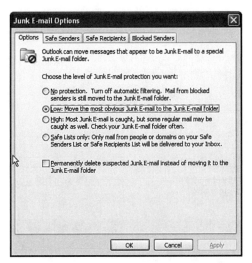

**Figure 6.57** The Junk E-mail Options dialog box.

**Figure 6.58** Configuring the Trusted Senders list.

# Blocking Junk Email

Outlook's built-in junk email filter blocks messages using two methods: the Junk E-Mail Lists and a new feature that determines whether an email is junk based on the message structure and other properties. This new filter is enabled by default.

## To view and modify junk email settings:

1. Choose Tools > Options, and click the Junk E-mail button.

   The Junk E-mail Options dialog box appears.

2. Click the Options tab. Select the level of protection desired, or turn it off completely by choosing No Protection (**Figure 6.57**).

3. Click the Safe Senders tab. Click the Add button and type the email address or domain name of the senders whose messages you do not want to be filtered as junk email.

   You can also remove a selection from the Safe Senders list by selecting an entry and clicking Remove (**Figure 6.58**).

4. Click the Safe Recipients tab. Click the Add button and type the target email address or domain for messages you do not want to be filtered as junk email.

   In other words, the Safe Recipients tab lets you identify acceptable messages based on the address or domain to which they are sent. You can also remove a selection from the Safe Recipients list by choosing Remove.

5. Click the Blocked Senders tab and click Add to add individual addresses or domains whose messages you want to explicitly block.

6. Click OK to close the Junk E-Mail Options dialog box.

## ✔ Tips

- Although advanced, the Junk E-Mail filter is not 100% effective. Periodically check the messages that are filtered to ensure that the filter is working properly.

- The Safe Senders list serves as a *whitelist* that identifies messages that should not be treated as junk, based on the address or domain of the sender. Use this list to allow incoming messages from known senders or domains, regardless of the message content. If you specify a domain, Outlook accepts all messages from that domain regardless of the sender.

- The Safe Recipients list serves as a whitelist that identifies messages that should not be treated as junk, based on the address to which the message is sent (or the domain of the address to which it is sent). Use this list to allow incoming messages that are not addressed specifically to you, such as messages sent to a discussion list in which you participate.

- The Blocked Senders list is a *blacklist* that explicitly identifies individual senders or domains whose messages you want Outlook to block.

- You can import or export a standard text file into the Safe Senders, Safe Recipients, or Blocked Senders list to share the list with other users or move it to another computer. To export a list, click Export to File in the Junk E-mail Options dialog box, specify the file path and name, and click Save. To import a list, click Import from File in the Junk E-mail Options dialog box. You see the Import Blocked Senders dialog box (**Figure 6.59**). Browse to the text file location, select it, and click Open. Outlook will import it into the list (**Figure 6.60**).

**Figure 6.59** Importing addresses in the Blocked Senders list.

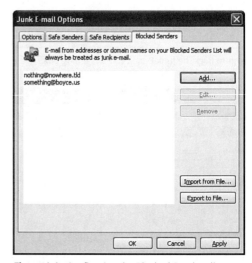

**Figure 6.60** Configuring the Blocked Senders list.

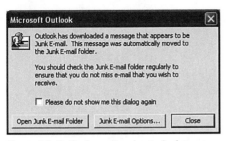

Figure 6.61 Outlook warning about a junk message.

- When Outlook receives a message it identifies as junk mail, it displays a warning message (**Figure 6.61**). Click Open Junk E-mail folder to view the junk email contents or Junk E-mail Options to view the filter configuration settings. Click Close to close the dialog box without taking any action.

# USING THE CALENDAR

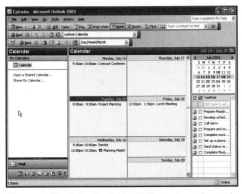

**Figure 7.1** The Calendar folder in the commonly used Day/Week/Month view, showing one week.

You can use your Calendar folder to maintain your personal schedule or to schedule meetings with others (**Figure 7.1**). The Calendar folder stores three types of items:

◆ **Appointments**. An appointment is an activity that consumes a block of your time—for example, an interview that you will conduct on Monday, your daily lunch break, or your weekly chess game.

◆ **Events**. An event is an occurrence that lasts one or more complete days, but doesn't fully consume your time—for example, your birthday, a holiday, or casual dress day at your company.

◆ **Meetings**. A meeting is like an appointment, but it includes other people or resources that you schedule using Outlook.

In this book, calendar item is the general term used to refer to any of these items.

In this chapter, you'll learn how to:

◆ Create appointments

◆ Define events

◆ Schedule meetings

◆ Work with items in the Calendar folder when viewing a day, a week, or a month

◆ Set Calendar folder options

◆ Create and view group schedules

## ✔ Tip

■ The techniques given in this chapter apply to the default Calendar folder as well as to any new calendar-item folders that you've created.

# Creating Appointments

You can create either a one-time appointment or a recurring appointment. A recurring appointment is one that occurs at regular intervals—daily, weekly, monthly, or yearly.

## To create a one-time appointment:

1. Open the Calendar folder.

2. Click the New button on the Standard toolbar, or choose Actions > New Appointment, or press Ctrl+N.

   Outlook will open an Appointment form (**Figure 7.2**).

3. Describe the appointment by entering information into the fields in the Appointment form:

   ▲ Enter a brief description of the appointment in the Subject text box and, if you wish, a more detailed description in the large text box.

   ▲ Type the appointment location in the Location list box, or from the drop-down list select a location that you've previously entered.

   ▲ Type the appointment starting date in the first Start Time list box, or click the down-arrow and select a date from the drop-down calendar (**Figure 7.3**). Type the appointment starting time in the second Start Time list box or select a time from the drop-down list (**Figure 7.4**).

   ▲ In a similar manner, specify the appointment ending date and time in the two End Time list boxes.

**Figure 7.2** A blank Appointment form for defining a new appointment.

**Figure 7.3** Selecting an appointment starting date from the drop-down calendar.

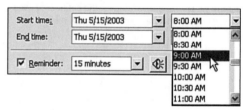

**Figure 7.4** Selecting an appointment starting time from the drop-down list.

*Reminder Sound button*

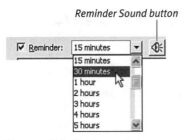

**Figure 7.5** Selecting the reminder time from the drop-down list.

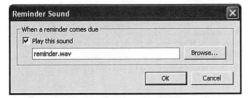

**Figure 7.6** The Reminder Sound dialog box.

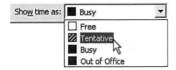

**Figure 7.7** Selecting the way Outlook will mark the appoint-ment in the Calendar folder.

▲ If you want Outlook to display a reminder message box just before the appointment starting time, check the Reminder option. Also, specify the amount of time before the start of the appointment that the reminder is to be displayed. You can do this by typing a time in the list box or selecting a time from the drop-down list (**Figure 7.5**). If you want to turn the reminder sound off or on or to select a different sound, click the Reminder Sound button to open the Reminder Sound dialog box (**Figure 7.6**).

▲ To indicate how the time will be marked in your Calendar folder (see the second tip in the following set), select an item from the Show Time As list box (**Figure 7.7**).

▲ If a contact in your Contacts folder is associated with the appointment (for example, the person you're going to be meeting), type the contact's name in the Contacts text box, or click the Contacts button to select that contact from your Contacts folder. This will link the appointment to the contact. You'll then be able to open the contact by double-clicking the name in the Contacts list box. Also, the Activities tab of the Contact form for that contact will list the appointment, along with any other linked Outlook items.

*continues on next page*

**CREATING APPOINTMENTS**

▲ If you want to assign a category to the appointment, type it in the Categories text box, or click the Categories button to select a category from the Categories dialog box (**Figure 7.8**). You can use a category to sort, filter, group, or find appointments (these operations are discussed in Chapter 3, "Working with Outlook Items").

▲ If you're sharing your Calendar folder but you want the appointment to be hidden, check the Private option. (Sharing folders is discussed in the "Sharing Outlook Folders over a Network" section in Chapter 4, "Working with Outlook Folders.")

A completed Appointment form is shown in **Figure 7.9**.

4. Click the Save And Close button on the form's Standard toolbar to save your new appointment in the Calendar folder and to close the Appointment form.

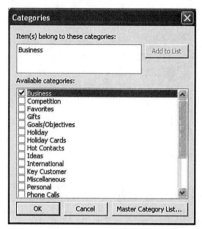

**Figure 7.8** Selecting one or more categories for an appointment in the Categories dialog box.

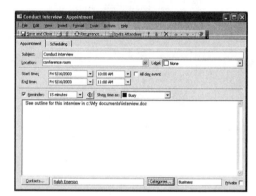

**Figure 7.9** A completed Appointment form.

## ✔ Tips

- You can quickly specify the starting and ending dates and times for an appointment by selecting the time in the Day/Week/Month view of the Calendar folder prior to opening the Appointment form. You select times just like you select items.

- When you display a single day or work week in the Day/Week/Month view of the Calendar folder, Outlook color-codes the border around each appointment according to your selection in the Show Time As list box, as follows: Free is white, Tentative is striped blue, Busy is dark blue, and Out Of Office is dark magenta.

- You can enter several names in the Contacts or Categories text boxes. If you type the names, separate them using commas or semicolons.

- Clicking the Invite Attendees toolbar button, or choosing Actions > Invite Attendees, or adding one or more attendees on the Scheduling tab converts the appointment into a meeting, which is described in "Scheduling Meetings," later in the chapter.

CREATING APPOINTMENTS

## To create a recurring appointment:

1. Open the Calendar folder.

2. Choose Actions > New Recurring Appointment.

   Outlook will open the Appointment Recurrence dialog box (**Figure 7.10**).

3. Define the appointment time, recurrence pattern, and range of recurrence by selecting options in the Appointment Recurrence dialog box. Click the OK button when you're done.

   Outlook will now open an Appointment form. The form will be the same as the one used for defining a one-time appointment, but will lack the fields for setting the starting and ending dates and times (**Figure 7.11**), because with a recurring appointment, all dates and times are set in the Appointment Recurrence dialog box.

4. Describe the appointment by entering information into the fields on the Appointment form, following the instructions given in "To create a one-time appointment," earlier in the chapter.

5. Click the Save And Close toolbar button to save your new recurring appointment in the Calendar folder and to close the Appointment form.

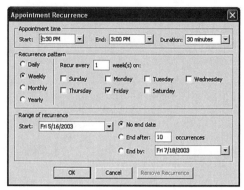

**Figure 7.10** The Appointment Recurrence dialog box.

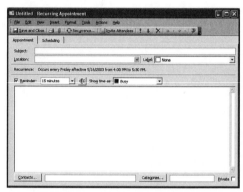

**Figure 7.11** The Appointment form for a recurring appointment.

**Figure 7.12** The message box Outlook shows when you open an instance of a recurring appointment.

## ✔ Tips

■ To change an appointment's recurrence information or to remove the recurrence, reopen the Appointment Recurrence dialog box by clicking the Recurrence toolbar button or choosing Actions > Recurrence on the Appointment form. To remove the recurrence, thereby converting the appointment to a one-time appointment, click the Remove Recurrence button in the Appointment Recurrence dialog box.

■ Clicking the Recurrence toolbar button, or choosing Actions > Recurrence, or pressing Ctrl+G opens the Appointment Recurrence dialog box, which lets you convert a one-time appointment into a recurring appointment.

■ If you open an occurrence of a recurring appointment to view or edit it, Outlook will give you the opportunity to open the specific occurrence or to open (and thereby modify) the appointment information for the entire series (**Figure 7.12**). Edit the occurrence if you want to change the appointment only for that one date, or edit the series to make global changes for all dates.

# Defining Events

As with an appointment, you can define either a one-time event or a recurring event. The following procedure shows you how to define either type of event.

### To define an event:

1. Open the Calendar folder.

2. Choose Actions > New All Day Event. Outlook will open the Event form (**Figure 7.13**). The form lets you specify starting and ending dates, but not specific starting and ending times (that's because an event always lasts one or more complete days).

3. Describe the event by entering information into the fields in the Event form, following the instructions for entering information into the Appointment form given in "To create a one-time appointment," earlier in the chapter. Be sure to leave the All Day Event button checked (otherwise the event will be converted to an appointment).

4. If you want to create a recurring event, click the Recurrence toolbar button or choose Actions > Recurrence, and in the Appointment Recurrence dialog box define the event time, recurrence pattern, and range of recurrence (see **Figure 7.10**, earlier in the chapter).

5. Click the Save And Close toolbar button to save your new event in the Calendar folder and to close the Event form.

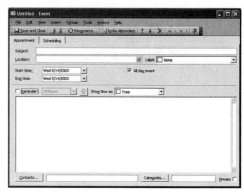

**Figure 7.13** The Event form.

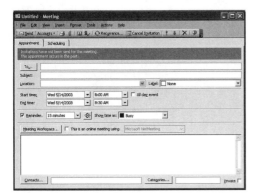

**Figure 7.14** The Meeting form.

**Figure 7.15** Selecting the Attendees and Resources.

# Scheduling Meetings

You can use Outlook to schedule meetings with other people. When you do this, Outlook stores a meeting item in your Calendar folder, and it sends copies of the meeting item to the people you invite.

## ✔ Tip

■ Scheduling a meeting allows you to share a specific calendar item (a meeting) with other people. Keep in mind that you can also share an entire Calendar folder with other people using the techniques discussed in "Sharing Outlook Folders over a Network" in Chapter 4.

## To schedule a meeting:

1. Open the Calendar folder.

2. Choose Actions > New Meeting Request, or press Ctrl+Shift+Q.

   Outlook will open the Meeting form (**Figure 7.14**), which is the same as an Appointment form except that it includes a To button and a text box.

3. Click the To button to display the Select Attendees and Resources dialog box (**Figure 7.15**).

4. Select an attendee and click Required if the attendee must attend the meeting or click Optional if the attendee is not required.

   To include a resource, such as a conference room, piece of equipment, or an assistant, select the person or item and click Resources.

5. Click OK to return to the meeting request form.

*continues on next page*

**6.** Describe the meeting by entering information into the fields on the Meeting form, following the instructions given in "To create a one-time appointment," earlier in the chapter.

**7.** If you want to create a recurring meeting, which is analogous to a recurring appointment, click the Recurrence toolbar button or choose Actions > Recurrence, and in the Appointment Recurrence dialog box define the meeting time, recurrence pattern, and range of recurrence (see **Figure 7.10**, earlier in the chapter). (You can also create a recurring meeting by choosing Actions > New Recurring Meeting to open the form in step 2.)

**Figure 7.16** shows a completed Meeting form.

**8.** Click the Send toolbar button.

Outlook will save the meeting in your Calendar folder, close the Meeting form, and send a meeting request to each attendee.

The meeting request will appear in the Inbox of each attendee. An attendee can reply by opening the request and clicking the Accept, Tentative, or Decline toolbar button (**Figure 7.17**). If an attendee clicks the Accept or Tentative button, the meeting is added to his or her Calendar folder (**Figure 7.18**) and the meeting request moves to the Deleted Items folder.

The attendee also has the option to recommend an alternate time by clicking the Propose New Time toolbar button, if for some reason, the original time is not adequate.

When an attendee replies, the response is sent back to you by email, and Outlook records the response in the original meeting item in your Calendar folder.

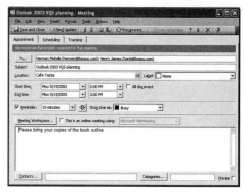

**Figure 7.16** A completed Meeting form, ready to send to attendees.

*Accept* ——*Tentative* *Decline*

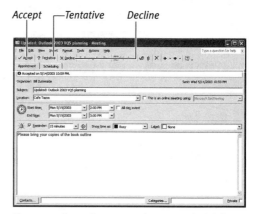

**Figure 7.17** A meeting request in an attendee's Inbox.

*Propose New Time*

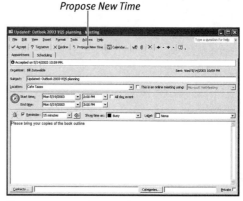

**Figure 7.18** A meeting item that was automatically added to an attendee's Calendar folder.

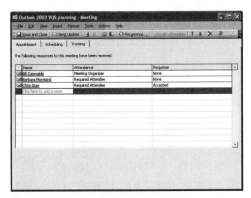

**Figure 7.19** Viewing the responses from the meeting attendees.

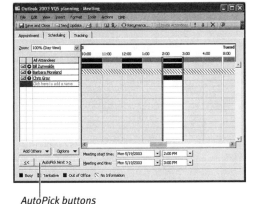

*AutoPick buttons*

**Figure 7.20** Displaying the Scheduling information.

**9.** If you want to see which attendees have replied and to view their responses, open the meeting item in your Calendar folder, open the Tracking tab to display the attendee response status (**Figure 7.19**).

**10.** To view the current attendees' schedules and how the meeting request correlates with the attendees' calendar, click the Scheduling tab in your Calendar folder (**Figure 7.20**). Use the fields to modify the meeting, such as changing start and stop times and adding attendees.

## ✔ Tips

■ If an attendee doesn't use Outlook but has an email program that supports the standard *iCalendar* format, you should send the meeting request in this format by choosing Tools > Send As iCalendar in the form (don't choose the command if it's checked, indicating that the option is already on).

■ Scheduling meetings won't work as you might expect if you or an attendee use an email service that doesn't transmit the required information. In this case, the attendee will receive a meeting request email message, but the form won't display the Accept or Decline buttons. To overcome this limitation and simplify response by attendees, forward the request in iCalendar format (see next tip).

■ You can send a meeting request to different attendees using different formats as needed. For example, create the meeting request and then choose Actions > Forward As iCalendar. Specify the users who need the iCalendar format and click Send. Outlook then returns to the original meeting request form, which you can address for all other users, and click Send in that form to send them the invitation.

*continues on next page*

■ Checking the All Day Event option on
the Meeting form converts the meeting
to an invited event, which is an event to
which others are invited. For example,
you might do this for an all-day meeting
or to invite others to a trade show or all-
day demonstration.

■ Clicking the Cancel Invitation toolbar
button or choosing Actions > Cancel
Invitation on the Meeting form converts
the meeting into an appointment (or an
event if All Day Event is checked). You
might do this if you decide that you do
not need to invite the other individuals
by email to the appointment.

■ If all your attendees have published their
free/busy schedules on the Internet or on
an Exchange Server network, you can
open the Scheduling tab on the Meeting
form and use the fields to locate times
when all attendees are available for your
meeting. Type "schedule a meeting" in the
Office Assistant for more information.

■ The Microsoft Internet Free/Busy Service
is a free service that enables Outlook
users without Exchange Server to share
their free/busy information with others.
These people can log onto the service
with a Web browser to your schedule.
Enrolling in the service requires a
Microsoft Passport, which associates
your identity with your email address. To
configure Outlook to use the service, or
just to learn more about it, choose Tools
> Options and click Calendar Options.
Click Free/Busy Options, enable the
option Publish and Search Using
Microsoft Office Internet Free/Busy
Service, and then click Manage. Outlook
opens your Web browser and navigates
to the service's Web site.

■ The AutoPick buttons on the Scheduling tab of the Meeting form (**Figure 7.20**) allow searching forward (AutoPick Next >>) and backward (<<) to find the next available time for all attendees who are available for the meeting. For example, if the meeting is two hours, the AutoPick Next >> button will find the first available two-hour time block ahead of your selection that all attendees have open.

■ If the meeting is going to be an online meeting using Microsoft NetMeeting, Windows Media Services, or Microsoft Exchange Conferencing, check the This Is an Online Meeting Using option and select the online meeting software you're using from the adjoining list (**Figure 7.21**). When you check This Is an Online Meeting Using, the Appointment form displays several additional fields for which you'll need to make selections (the particular options you see depend upon the online meeting software you select). Enter the name of the directory server in the Directory Server text box or click the down arrow to select from existing servers.

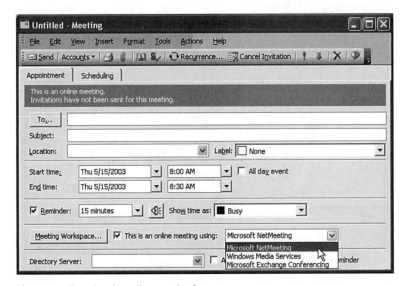

**Figure 7.21** Choosing the online meeting format.

# Working with Items in the Calendar Folder

The most commonly used view of the Calendar folder is Day/Week/Month, which displays your appointments, events, and meetings in a typical calendar or day planner format. In this view, you can display a single day, a work week, a full week, or a month.

## ✔ Tips

- If you want to publish your Calendar folder on the Internet, you can save it as a Web page by choosing File > Save As Web Page and selecting options in the Save As Web Page dialog box (**Figure 7.22**).

- You can resize or remove any of the panes in the Day/Week/Month view (the time list, the Date Navigator, or the TaskPad) by dragging the appropriate border between panes.

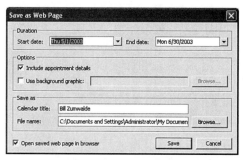

**Figure 7.22** The Save As Web Page dialog box.

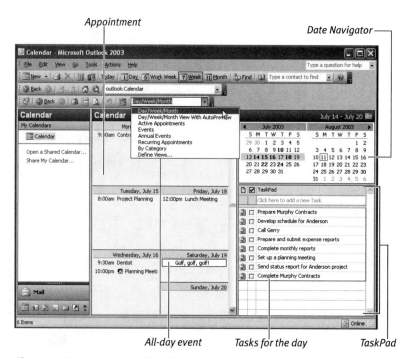

**Figure 7.23** Selecting the Day/Week/Month view.

## To work with a single day:

**1.** Activate the Day/Week/Month view of the Calendar folder (**Figure 7.23**).

**2.** Click the Day button on the Standard toolbar, or choose View > Day.

Outlook will initially display the current day, in a day planner format (see **Figure 7.18** earlier in this chapter).

**3.** To view a particular day, click that date in the Date Navigator (**Figure 7.24**).

**4.** To add a new appointment, click the desired appointment time and type the appointment subject in the box.

*or*

Double-click the time to open a blank Appointment form. (See "Creating Appointments" at the beginning of this chapter.)

All-day event    Appointment        Date Navigator

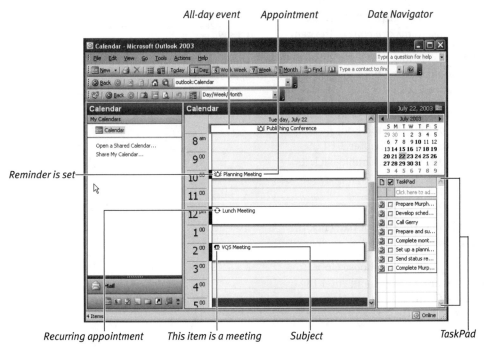

Reminder is set

Recurring appointment    This item is a meeting    Subject        TaskPad

**Figure 7.24** The Date Navigator.

*continues on next page*

**5.** To add a new event, click in the banner at the top of the list of times (but not on an existing event) and type the event subject.

*or*

Double-click in the banner (but not on an existing event) to open a blank Event form (**Figure 7.25**).

**6.** To edit an item's subject, click within the item to select it. Outlook will display a thick border around the item, and will place the insertion point within the subject text so you can edit it.

**7.** To change an item's time, drag the item to a new time slot within the same day.

*or*

To move the item to a different date, drag the item to that date in the Date Navigator, keeping the time the same.

If the item is already selected, drag the item's left border (**Figure 7.26**). Press Ctrl while you drag to make a copy of the item.

**8.** To change a calendar item's duration, drag the item's bottom border up or down (**Figure 7.27**).

**9.** To open an item in a form, double-click it or use any of the other methods given in "To open an item" in Chapter 3. (If the item is already selected, double-click its border.)

### ✔ Tips

■ To quickly view the current day, click the Today button on the Standard toolbar.

■ To view a specific date, choose Go > Go To Date, or press Ctrl+G, and enter the date in the Go To Date dialog box.

*Double-click in the banner*

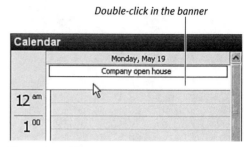

**Figure 7.25** Adding a new event.

*Drag here to move a selected item*

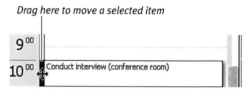

**Figure 7.26** Moving a selected item.

*Drag up or down to shorten or lengthen the appointment*

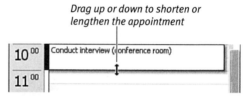

**Figure 7.27** Changing the duration of an appointment.

*Work Week button*

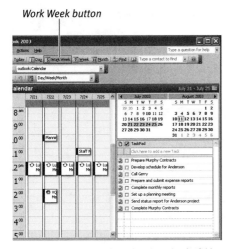

**Figure 7.28** Viewing a work week in the Calendar folder.

*Week button*

**Figure 7.29** Viewing an entire week in the Calendar folder.

*Click here to view the week beginning May 11*

**Figure 7.30** Selecting a week to view.

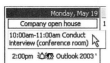

**Figure 7.31** Viewing the full item text in a ScreenTip.

## To work with a week:

1. Activate the Day/Week/Month view of the Calendar folder.

2. To view a work week (Monday through Friday) (**Figure 7.28**), click the Work Week button on the Standard toolbar, or choose View > Work Week.

   *or*

   To view a full week (Monday through Sunday) (**Figure 7.29**), click the Week button on the Standard toolbar or choose View > Week.

3. Work with the items using the techniques given in the previous section, "To work with a single day," but keep in mind the following:

   ▲ To view a particular week, click to the left of the week in the Date Navigator (**Figure 7.30**).

   ▲ If you're viewing a full week, clicking a day and typing a subject adds an event, and double-clicking a day opens an Event form.

   ▲ If you're viewing a full week, you can drag an item to a different day, but to change an item's time or duration, you have to open the item and edit the times on the form.

## ✔ Tip

■ If the text for an item is cut off, you can point to the item and view the full text in a ScreenTip (**Figure 7.31**).

**WORKING WITH ITEMS IN THE CALENDAR FOLDER**

## To work with a month:

1. Activate the Day/Week/Month view of the Calendar folder.

2. Click the Month button on the Standard toolbar, or choose View > Month.

   Outlook will initially display the current month in a standard calendar format (**Figure 7.32**).

3. To view a different month, use the vertical scroll bar to scroll through the months (**Figure 7.33**), or pick a month in the Date Navigator by clicking and holding the left mouse button down on the month title bar and scrolling up or down. Release the mouse button to choose a month (**Figure 7.34**).

   If the Date Navigator is hidden, drag the border at the right of the window toward the left.

4. Work with the items using the techniques given in the earlier section, "To work with a single day," but keep in mind the following:

   ▲ Clicking on a day and typing a subject adds an event; double-clicking a day opens an Event form.

   ▲ You can drag an item to a different day, but to change its time or duration, you have to open the item and edit the times in the form.

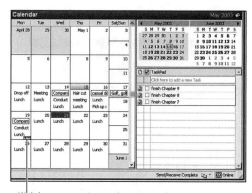

Click here to see items that aren't shown

**Figure 7.32** Displaying a month in the Calendar folder.

Click to view the previous month

Click to view the next month

**Figure 7.33** Selecting a month in the Date Navigator.

**Figure 7.34** Selecting a month in the drop-menu.

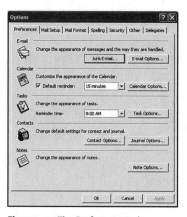

**Figure 7.35** The Preferences tab of the Options dialog box.

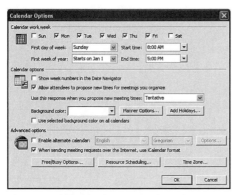

**Figure 7.36** The Calendar Options dialog box.

*Change the Date Navigator font*

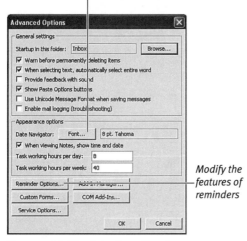

*Modify the features of reminders*

**Figure 7.37** Setting Calendar options in the Advanced Options dialog box.

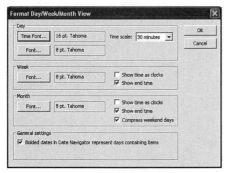

**Figure 7.38** The Format Day/Week/ Month View dialog box for changing features of the Day/Week/Monthly view of the Calendar folder.

## To set Calendar options:

◆ To have Outlook display a reminder message by default for the new calendar items you create, choose Tools > Options; on the Preferences tab check Default Reminder, and select the default reminder time in the adjoining text box (**Figure 7.35**). (This is only a default setting. If you wish, you can turn off the reminder for a particular calendar item.)

◆ To change the Calendar work week, to modify the Date Navigator, to change the Calendar background color, or to make other changes, click the Calendar Options button in the Preferences tab of the Options dialog box (**Figure 7.35**) and select the desired options in the Calendar Options dialog box (**Figure 7.36**).

◆ To change the font used in the Date Navigator or to modify the features of reminders, choose Tools > Options, open the Other tab, click the Advanced Options button, and select options in the Advanced Options dialog box (**Figure 7.37**).

◆ To modify features of the currently active view of the Calendar folder, choose View > Arrange By > Current View > Customize Current View, click the Other Settings button, and select the desired options in the Other Settings or Format Day/Week/Month View dialog box (**Figure 7.38**). (The name and contents of the dialog box vary according to the current view.)

# Creating and Viewing Group Schedules

Group schedules are a logical grouping created to help manage groups of people and/or resources regardless of whether they are members of a Microsoft Exchange Server, on your intranet, or on the Internet. You can create and view a group schedule without creating a meeting. For example, assume you manage a sales department and you want to see which times of the day are the busiest for your sales staff. Or, perhaps you need to schedule maintenance and want to check availability of the resource at a given time to assign maintenance for it.

You can create multiple group schedules to view and manage time for multiple groups of users or resources. The advantage of this feature is the ability to store group schedules by name and manage them without needing to create a meeting request. Use group schedules when you want to manage time but not necessarily schedule meetings, or when you frequently need to create meeting requests for the same groups of people or resources. Start a new meeting request in those situations where you need to create a one-off meeting request.

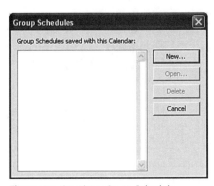

Figure 7.39 Creating a Group Schedule.

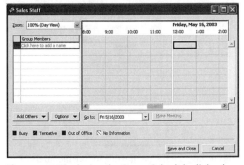

Figure 7.40 Displaying the Group Schedule dialog box.

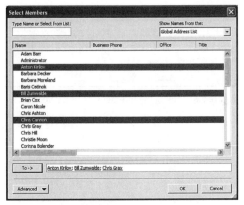

Figure 7.41 Selecting the members you want to add to the Group Schedule.

## To create and view a group schedule:

1. Choose Actions > View Group Schedules to display the Group Schedules box (**Figure 7.39**).

2. Click the New button to display the Create New Group Schedule dialog box, type a descriptive name, such as "Sales Staff," and click OK to display a dialog box with that group name (**Figure 7.40**).

3. Click the Add Others button, and select Add from Address Book to display the Select Members dialog box.

4. Select an address list in the drop-down list called Show Names From The (**Figure 7.41**), and select the members you want to add.

    If you then want to send messages to the members you chose, you can follow the instructions given in "To address a message" in Chapter 6.

5. Click OK to create the group and display the new group schedule "Sales Staff" (**Figure 7.42**).

*continues on next page*

## ✔ Tips

- If a member of a group schedule does not have an available schedule, it will display No Information, such as for Anton Kirlov in **Figure 7.42**.

- Click Add Others to add any combination of members from other sources, such as LDAP servers, your Outlook Contacts, or public folders.

- The Make Meeting button (**Figure 7.43**) allows creation of meetings and other options such as New Mail Message with All, which opens a message form with the group members already selected in the To field.

- Group Schedule membership does not prohibit membership in another group schedules and deletion of a member only deletes that person or resource from the group.

- If you are not currently a member of a Free/Busy service, you will be prompted to join (**Figure 7.44**) when creating a Group Schedule.

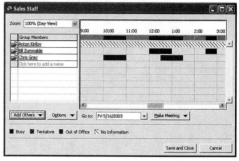

**Figure 7.42** Displaying the Group Schedule.

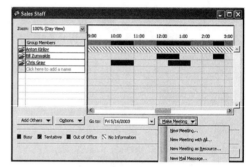

**Figure 7.43** Creating a meeting for the members of the new Group.

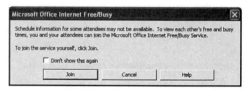

**Figure 7.44** Joining the Internet Free/Busy Service.

# Using the
# Contact Folder

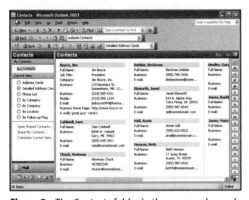

**Figure 8.1** The Contacts folder in the commonly used Address Cards view.

You can use your Contacts folder to store information about friends, business associates, and companies. This information can include a name; a title; a company name; a Web page address; several street addresses, phone numbers, email addresses; and many other pieces of information (**Figure 8.1**).

You can use the items in your Contacts folder to look up information on people or companies, to send them email, to dial their phone numbers, to visit their Web sites, or to contact them in other ways.

In this chapter, you'll learn how to:

◆ Create a new contact item: either a contact or a distribution list

◆ Find a contact

◆ Send a message to a contact, dial a contact's phone number, visit a contact's Web site, and reach a contact in other ways

◆ Set options for the Contacts folder

## ✔ Tip

■ You can use most of the instructions given in this chapter either with the default Contacts folder or with another contact-item folder that you've created.

# Creating Contact Items

You can create two different types of items in your Contacts folder (**Figure 8.2**):

◆ A **contact**, which stores information on a single person or company.

◆ A **distribution list**, which stores a list of names and addresses or fax numbers. You can use a distribution list to send an email or fax message, a meeting request, or a task assignment to an entire group of people (for example, everyone in your workgroup). To address one of these items to the group, you select the name of the distribution list rather than selecting or entering an individual address.

## To create a contact:

1. Open the Contacts folder.

2. Click the New button on the Standard toolbar, or choose Actions > New Contact, or press Ctrl+N.

   Outlook will open a Contact form (**Figure 8.3**).

3. Enter the desired information into the fields on the General tab of the Contact form:

   ▲ Type the contact's full name in the Full Name text box (see the first tip in the following set).

   ▲ Type the contact's job title and company (if any) in the Job Title and Company text boxes.

   ▲ Use the Address text box to enter up to three street or post office box addresses, as shown in **Figure 8.4** (see the first tip in the following set).

   ▲ If the contact receives mail at the address shown in the Address text box, check the This is the Mailing Address option.

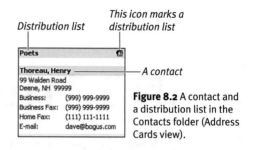

*Distribution list* — *This icon marks a distribution list*

*A contact*

**Figure 8.2** A contact and a distribution list in the Contacts folder (Address Cards view).

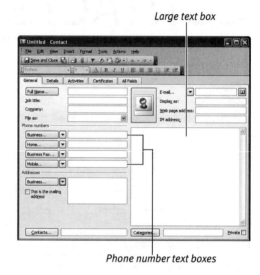

*Large text box*

*Phone number text boxes*

**Figure 8.3** A Contact form, ready to define a new contact.

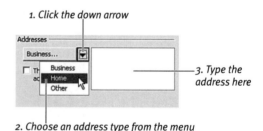

*1. Click the down arrow*

*3. Type the address here*

*2. Choose an address type from the menu*

**Figure 8.4** Entering a street or post office box address.

*1. Click the down arrow*

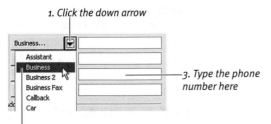

*2. Choose a phone number type from the drop-down menu*

*3. Type the phone number here*

**Figure 8.5** Entering a phone number in one of the phone number text boxes.

*1. Click the down arrow*

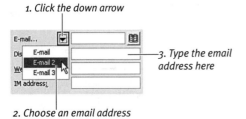

*2. Choose an email address*

*3. Type the email address here*

**Figure 8.6** Entering an email address.

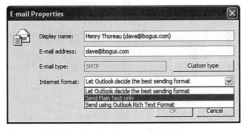

**Figure 8.7** Selecting the Internet format.

**Figure 8.8** Resting the mouse over a smart tag.

▲ Use the Phone Numbers text boxes to enter up to four phone numbers, as shown in **Figure 8.5**.

▲ Use the E-mail text box to enter up to three email addresses for the contact, as shown in **Figure 8.6** (see the second tip in the following set).

▲ If the contact's email service or software doesn't support the Rich Text or HTML email format, double-click on the email address to open the E-mail Properties dialog box. Click the drop-down list and select the Send Plain Text Only option (**Figure 8.7**) so that all email messages will be sent to the contact in plain text.

▲ If the contact has a Web site, type the full address of the home page in the Web Page Address text box.

▲ If you want to enter any general information (such as instructions on finding the contact's house), type it in the large text box.

▲ If you want to link another contact to the current contact, type the other contact's name in the Contacts text box or click the Contacts button to select that contact from your Contacts folder. You'll then be able to open the other contact by double-clicking the name in the Contacts list box. Also, the Activities tab of the Contact form for the other contact will list the current contact, along with any other linked Outlook items.

▲ Rest the mouse pointer over the contact name and click on the icon that appears to select actions for that contact (**Figure 8.8**).

*continues on next page*

CREATING CONTACT ITEMS

▲ If you want to assign a category to the contact, type it in the Categories text box or click the Categories button to select a category from the Categories dialog box (**Figure 8.9**). You can use a category to sort, filter, group, or find contacts. (These operations are discussed in Chapter 3, "Working with Outlook Items.")

▲ If you're sharing your Contacts folder but you want the contact to be hidden, check the Private option. (Sharing folders is discussed in "Sharing Outlook Folders over a Network" in Chapter 4, "Working with Outlook Folders.")

▲ To add a picture to the contact form, select the picture icon (**Figure 8.10**) to open the Add Contact Picture browser window. Browse to the picture and click OK.

▲ If the contact uses instant messaging, enter their address in the IM Address field. If the person is already added to your Windows Messaging contact list, you don't need to add this entry. Add this entry only if the person's IM address is different from his email address. Adding this entry enables you to view IM status for the person with the Person Names smart tag, which appears beside the sender's name in the Reading pane when you click the header of a message from that person. See the section, "Using Instant Messaging with Outlook," later in this chapter for more details.

4. To enter the contact's department, office, profession, nickname, and other less commonly used information, open the Details tab.

**Figure 8.11** shows a completed Contact form.

**Figure 8.9** Selecting one or more categories for a contact in the Categories dialog box.

**Figure 8.10** Selecting the picture icon to add a picture to the contact form.

**Figure 8.11** A completed Contact form.

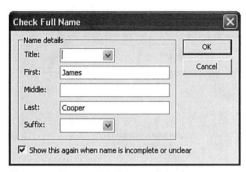

**Figure 8.12** The Check Full Name dialog box.

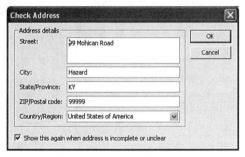

**Figure 8.13** The Check Address dialog box.

**5.** Click the Save And Close button on the form's Standard toolbar to save the new contact in the Contacts folder and to close the form.

## ✔ Tips

■ Outlook divides the name and the address you type into separate fields, such as first name and last name or street and city. You can sort, filter, group, search, or perform other operations using these individual fields. To see how Outlook has divided the name or address you typed—and to make corrections if necessary—click the Full Name or "address" button (where "address" may be labeled Business, Home, or Other) to display the Check Full Name (**Figure 8.12**) or Check Address (**Figure 8.13**) dialog box. You can click the drop-down button beside the Address button to choose a specific address. Outlook will show one of these dialog boxes automatically if the name or address you type appears to be incorrectly formatted.

■ Entering an email address in the E-mail text box uses the same basic techniques as entering an email address in the To text box of a message. For instructions, see "To address a message" in Chapter 6, "Using the Inbox to Manage Messages."

■ You can enter several names in the Contacts or Categories text boxes. If you type the names, separate them using commas or semicolons.

CREATING CONTACT ITEMS

# Using Instant Messaging with Outlook

Outlook has the capability to integrate with instant messaging (IM) services such as MSN Messaging, Windows Messenger Service, and the Microsoft Exchange Instant Messaging Service. This feature allows you to see online status and communicate with people in your contacts list and Inbox using *Smart Tags*. Smart Tags work in real time with your contacts' instant messaging service to make IM commands and status easily accessible.

For example, you can see a contact's online/offline status. Move the mouse over the Contacts name to display the Smart Tag icon to the left of the contact (**Figure 8.14**). Move the mouse over the Smart Tag icon to display its online status (**Figure 8.15**). To communicate with the contact in real time, click on the Smart Tag icon and choose Send Instant Message (**Figure 8.16**) or select from several other options such as Schedule a Meeting or Send Mail (**Figure 8.17**)

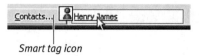

*Smart tag icon*

**Figure 8.14** Mouse over a contact to display a Smart Tag.

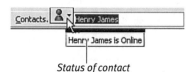

*Status of contact*

**Figure 8.15** Mouse over a Smart Tag to display the contact's online status.

**Figure 8.16** Sending an Instant Message in real time.

**Figure 8.17** Displaying a list of Smart Tag options for the contact.

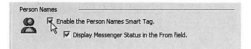

**Figure 8.18** Enabling the Person Names Smart Tag.

**Figure 8.19** Displaying a contact's online status in the Reading Pane.

## To enable Person Names Smart Tag:

1. Choose Tools > Options > Other.

2. Click the Enable the Person Names Smart Tag box (**Figure 8.18**).

   *or*

   Click Display Messenger Status in the From field to display smart tags in an email Reading Pane's From field (**Figure 8.19**). If the icon is green, the sender is online; red if not.

## ✔ Tip

■ If the Display Messenger Status in the From field option is disabled (grayed out), upgrade to the latest version of Windows Messenger to enable IM options in Outlook. You can obtain the latest version of Windows Messenger from the Windows Update site at http://windowsupdate.microsoft.com.

USING INSTANT MESSAGING WITH OUTLOOK

# Using Distribution Lists

Distribution lists enable you to address messages to multiple recipients more easily. Essentially, a distribution list is a named collection of email addresses. For example, you might create a distribution list named Sales that contains the email addresses of everyone in the Sales department or a list named Friends that contains the email addresses of the friends you email regularly. When you want to send an email to everyone in the list, you just add the distribution list to the email message To, Cc, or Bcc field rather than add all the individual addresses.

## To create a distribution list:

1. Open the Contacts folder.

2. Choose Actions > New Distribution List, or press Ctrl+Shift+L.

   Outlook will open a Distribution List form (**Figure 8.20**).

3. Define the distribution list by entering information into the fields:

   ▲ Type a name for the distribution list in the Name text box—for example, Marketing Department or Camera Club Members.

   ▲ To add one or more distribution list members by picking them from your Contacts folder, from another address list, or from an Internet directory service, click the Select Members button to open the Select Members dialog box (**Figure 8.21**). This dialog box works just like the Select Names dialog box used to address a message, and it varies according to your email configuration. For instructions, see "To address a message" in Chapter 6.

   ▲ To add a distribution list member by typing a new name and address, click the Add New button and fill in the Add New Member dialog box (**Figure 8.22**).

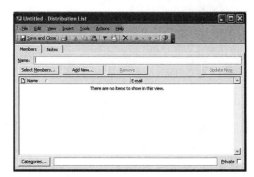

**Figure 8.20** A Distribution List form, ready to define a new distribution list.

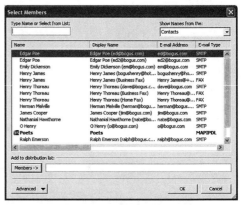

**Figure 8.21** The Select Members dialog box.

**Figure 8.22** The Add New Member dialog box.

**Figure 8.23** The dialog box displayed if Outlook cannot find a contact.

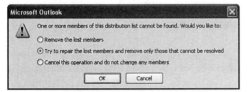

**Figure 8.24** The dialog box displayed if Outlook cannot find multiple contacts.

▲ To remove a member from the distribution list, select the name in the list and click the Remove button.

▲ If you want to assign a category to the distribution list, type it in the Categories text box, or click the Categories button to select a category from the Categories dialog box (see **Figure 8.9**, earlier in the chapter). You can use a category to sort, filter, group, or find distribution lists (these operations are discussed in Chapter 3).

▲ If you're sharing your Contacts folder but you want the distribution list to be hidden, check the Private option. (Sharing folders is discussed in "Sharing Outlook Folders over a Network" in Chapter 4.)

▲ If you want to type a description of the distribution list or enter any other information, open the Notes tab.

4. Click the Save And Close button on the form's Standard toolbar to save the new distribution list in the Contacts folder and close the form.

## ✔ Tips

■ If, after you create a distribution list, you delete a member contact or change a member contact's email address, you can update the information displayed on the Distribution List form by clicking the Update Now button. Outlook will display the dialog box shown in **Figure 8.23** if it cannot find a contact and prompt you to delete it. Outlook displays the message shown in **Figure 8.24** if it cannot find multiple contacts and prompts you to Remove the lost members, Try to repair the lost members and remove only those that cannot be resolved, or Cancel (the) operation and do not change any members.

■ You can enter several names in the Contacts or Categories text boxes. If you type the names, separate them using commas or semicolons.

# Working with Items in the Contacts Folder

In addition to the general ways of working with Outlook items that were discussed in Chapter 3, the Contacts folder provides some unique methods for working with contact items:

◆ In addition to using the standard Find pane or Advanced Find dialog box, you can quickly find a contact, regardless of which folder is open in Outlook, by using the Find a Contact list box on the Standard toolbar.

◆ You can use Actions menu commands to quickly "contact a contact" by sending the contact an email message or letter, calling the contact, opening the contact's Web site, or reaching the contact in other ways.

## To find a contact using the Find a Contact list box:

◆ In the Find a Contact list box on the Standard toolbar, type the first or last name or the email address of the contact you want to find (**Figure 8.25**) and press Enter. You don't need to enter the full name.

*or*

Select a previously entered search item from the drop-down list (**Figure 8.26**).

Outlook will now do one of the following:

▲ If it finds a unique matching contact, it will open it in a form.

▲ If it finds several matching contacts, it will let you choose one (**Figure 8.27**).

▲ If it doesn't find a match, it will tell you so (**Figure 8.28**).

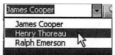

**Figure 8.25** Typing a contact name in the Find a Contact list box.

**Figure 8.26** Selecting a previous search item from the Find A Contact list box.

**Figure 8.27** Choosing the contact you want to open. (This dialog box was displayed after I typed **henry** in the Find a Contact list box.)

**Figure 8.28** The message box Outlook displays when it doesn't find a matching contact.

**Figure 8.29** The Dial button drop-down menu.

## To contact a contact:

1. Open the Contacts folder.

2. Select a contact or a distribution list.

3. Choose the command to carry out the desired action:

   ▲ To send an email to the contact or distribution list, click the New Message To Contact button on the Standard toolbar or choose Actions > New Message To Contact.

   ▲ To write a letter to the contact, choose Actions > New Letter To Contact. This command requires Microsoft Word and can be used only with a contact, not a distribution list.

   ▲ To send a meeting request to the contact or distribution list, click the New Meeting Request To Contact button on the Advanced toolbar, or choose Actions > New Meeting Request to Contact. See "Scheduling Meetings" in Chapter 7, "Using the Calendar."

   ▲ To call the contact, click the down arrow on the Dial button on the Standard toolbar and then choose a command from the drop-down menu (**Figure 8.29**), or choose Actions > Call Contact and then choose a command from the submenu. To use Outlook to call a contact, you must have a modem connected to the same line as your telephone.

   ▲ To call the contact using Microsoft NetMeeting, click the Call Using NetMeeting button on the Advanced toolbar or choose Actions > Call Using NetMeeting. You can use this command only for a contact, not a distribution list.

   *continues on next page*

▲ To display a contact's home page in your Web browser, click the Explore Web Page button on the Advanced toolbar. You can use this command only for a contact, not a distribution list.

## ✔ Tips

■ If a contact item is opened in a form, you can perform any of the actions in the preceding list by choosing commands on the form's Actions menu.

■ If a contact is opened in a form, you may be able to display a map of the contact's address by clicking the Display Map Of Address toolbar button or by choosing Actions > Display Map Of Address. Outlook will connect to the Microsoft Expedia Web site and attempt to find a map.

**Figure 8.30** The Contact Options dialog box.

**Figure 8.31** The Format Card View dialog box for changing features of the Address Cards view of the Contacts folder.

## To set Contacts options:

◆ To change the order in which you enter names for new contacts or the default way Outlook sorts contacts, choose Tools > Options. Click the Contact Options button on the Preferences tab and select the desired options in the Contact Options dialog box (**Figure 8.30**).

*or*

To modify features of the currently active view of the Contacts folder, choose View > Arrange By > Current View > Customize Current View. Click the Other Settings button, and select the desired options in the Other Settings dialog box (for a table view) or the Format Card View dialog box (for the Address Cards view) (**Figure 8.31**).

## ✔ Tip

■ In the Address Cards view, you can adjust the width of the cards by dragging one of the vertical separators between columns of cards, or you can double-click a separator to have Outlook adjust the card width so that an even number of columns will just fit within the Outlook window.

# USING THE TASKS FOLDER

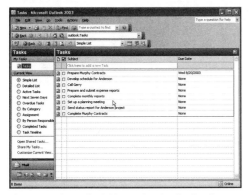

**Figure 9.1** The Tasks folder in the Simple List view.

You can use the Tasks folder to keep track of personal tasks that you need to complete or to manage projects that involve other people (**Figure 9.1**).

In this chapter, you'll learn how to:

- ◆ Create a personal task for tracking a job you have to complete yourself

- ◆ Create a task request for assigning a task to someone else

- ◆ Work with your personal and assigned tasks in the Tasks folder, in a table, or in a timeline

- ◆ Set options for the Tasks folder

## ✔ Tip

- ■ You might want to create a separate task-item folder for each of your main projects. The techniques given in this chapter apply to the default Tasks folder as well as to any new task-item folders that you've created.

# Creating Task Items

You can create two types of items in your Tasks folder (**Figure 9.2**):

♦ A **personal task**, which is stored in your own Tasks folder and is used for tracking a job you need to complete by yourself. You are the owner of a personal task.

♦ An **assigned task**, which you create and assign to someone else by sending that person a task request via email. The person who is assigned the task becomes its owner and is responsible for completing it. The task is stored in the owner's Tasks folder, although you can keep a copy in your own Tasks folder. Outlook will automatically update your copy whenever the owner modifies the task. To manage a group project, you can assign tasks to various members of your workgroup in this way.

♦ The icon to the left of "Pick up the chips for the picnic" in **Figure 9.2** indicates a personal task, whereas the icon to the left of "Meeting to review Chapter 9" (with the hand under it) indicates an assigned task.

## To create a personal task:

1. Open the Tasks folder.

2. Click the New button on the Standard toolbar, or choose Actions > New Task, or press Ctrl+N.

   Outlook will open a Task form (**Figure 9.3**).

3. Enter the desired information into the fields in the Task tab of the Task form:

   ▲ Type a brief task description into the Subject text box.

   ▲ If you want to enter a full task description or any other information, type it into the large text box.

*A personal task*

*An assigned task*

**Figure 9.2** A personal task and a copy of an assigned task in the Tasks folder (Simple List view).

*Large text box*          *Reminder Sound button*

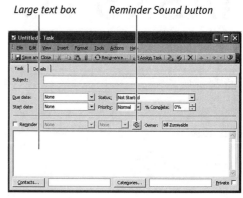

**Figure 9.3** A Task form, ready to define a new personal task.

Figure 9.4 Selecting a task due date.

Figure 9.5 Selecting the task's priority.

**Figure 9.6** The Reminder Sound dialog box.

▲ If the task is due on a particular date, type or select that date in the Due date list box (**Figure 9.4**). (If the task doesn't have a due date, leave None selected in the list box.)

▲ If the task is to be started on a particular date, type or select that date in the Start Date list box. (If the task doesn't have a specific starting date, leave None selected in the list box.)

▲ You generally leave Not Started selected in the Status list box and 0% in the % Complete text box, and then update these values later as you begin to make progress on the task.

▲ Specify the task's priority by selecting a value from the Priority list box (**Figure 9.5**).

▲ If you want Outlook to display a reminder message box before the task is due, check the Reminder option and type or select the date and the time that the reminder is to be displayed in the following two list boxes. Also, if you want to turn the reminder sound off or on, or select a different sound, click the Reminder Sound button to open the Reminder Sound dialog box (**Figure 9.6**).

▲ Make sure your name is displayed in the Owner text box, because you are the owner of a personal task. (If you assign the task to someone else, as described later, Outlook will change the owner for you.)

*continues on next page*

CREATING TASK ITEMS

▲ If a contact in your Contacts folder is associated with the task (for example, the client you're performing the task for), type the contact's name into the Contacts text box or click the Contacts button to select that contact from your Contacts folder. This will link the task to the contact. You'll then be able to open the contact by double-clicking the name. Also, the Activities tab of the Contact form for that contact will list the task along with any other linked Outlook items.

▲ If you want to assign a category to the task, type it into the Categories text box or click the Categories button to select a category from the Categories dialog box (**Figure 9.7**). You can use a category to sort, filter, group, or find tasks (these operations are discussed in Chapter 3, "Working with Outlook Items").

▲ If you're sharing your Tasks folder but you want the task to be hidden, check the Private option. (Sharing folders is discussed in the "Sharing Outlook Folders over a Network" section in Chapter 4, "Working with Outlook Folders.")

**Figure 9.8** shows a completed Task tab.

**4.** To further define the task, open the Details tab (**Figure 9.9**) and enter the desired information into the fields:

▲ Enter the estimated number of hours required to complete the task into the Total work text box.

▲ Enter appropriate information into the Mileage, Billing Information, and Companies text boxes.

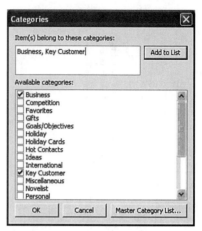

**Figure 9.7** The Categories dialog box.

**Figure 9.8** A completed Task tab.

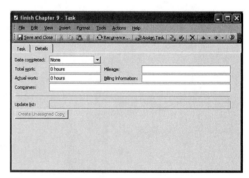

**Figure 9.9** The Details tab of the Task form.

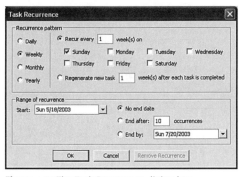

**Figure 9.10** The Task Recurrence dialog box.

▲ You normally don't enter information into the Date completed and Actual work fields until the task is completed.

▲ The Update list and Create Unassigned Copy fields are used only for assigned tasks, described later in the chapter.

5. If you want the task to be recurring, click the Recurrence toolbar button or choose Actions > Recurrence, and in the Task Recurrence dialog box define the recurrence pattern and range (**Figure 9.10**).

    A recurring task is a series of tasks (all with the same description and options) that are due on the dates that you specify. When you mark one task as completed, Outlook automatically generates the next task in the series and adds it to your Tasks folder.

6. Click the Save And Close toolbar button to save your new task in the Tasks folder and to close the form.

## ✔ Tips

■ You can enter several names into the Contacts or Categories text boxes. If you type the names, separate them using commas or semicolons.

■ With a recurring task, you can generate the next task without having to mark the current task as completed. To do this, open the task and choose Actions > Skip Occurrence in the form. The task's due date will be changed to the due date for the next task in the series.

■ Clicking the Assign Task toolbar button converts the personal task into an assigned task, as discussed next.

## To create an assigned task:

1. Open the Tasks folder.

2. Choose Actions > New Task Request, or press Ctrl+Shift+U.

   Outlook will open the Task form shown in **Figure 9.11**.

3. In the To text box, enter the address of the person you want to assign the task to. Follow the instructions given in the "To address a message" section in Chapter 6, "Using the Inbox to Manage Messages."

   The person to whom you assign the task becomes the task owner.

4. If you want to keep a copy of the assigned task in your own Tasks folder, check the Keep an Updated Copy of This Task on My Task List option.

   You won't be able to modify your copy of the task, but it will be updated automatically whenever the task owner modifies his or her copy.

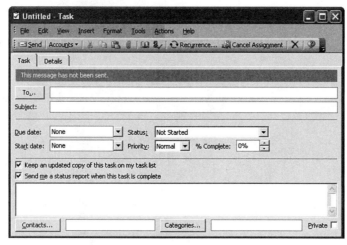

**Figure 9.11** A Task form, ready to define a new assigned task.

5. If you want to receive an email message when the task owner marks the task as completed, check the Send Me a Status Report When This Task Is Complete option.

6. Finish defining the task by entering information into the other fields in the Task and Details tabs. (Follow the instructions in "To create a personal task," earlier in the chapter.)

   Notice, however, that the Task tab doesn't contain fields for setting a reminder (only the task owner can set a reminder), nor does it contain an Owner text box (Outlook automatically assigns this field the name of the owner).

   **Figure 9.12** shows a completed Task form.

7. Click the Send button.

   Outlook will send the task to its owner, close the form, and (if you checked Send Me a Status Report When This Task Is Complete) save a copy of the task in your Tasks folder.

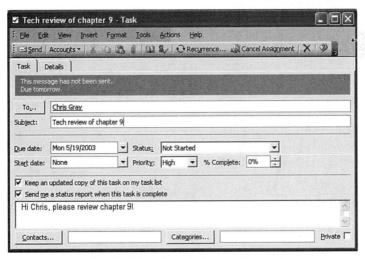

**Figure 9.12** A completed Task form for assigning a task to another person.

## When the owner receives the assigned task:

1. The owner receives the task request message in his or her Inbox (**Figure 9.13**).

2. The owner clicks the Accept or the Decline toolbar button in the task request form to take on or to refuse the task.

   In either case, you'll receive a message in your Inbox notifying you of the owner's response.

   ▲ If the owner clicked the Accept button, the task is added to his or her Tasks folder.

   ▲ If the owner clicked the Accept button and you originally checked the Send Me a Status Report When This Task Is Complete option, Outlook will automatically update your copy of the task whenever the owner modifies the task. (Outlook uses special email messages to keep your copy updated.)

   ▲ If the owner clicked the Accept button and you originally checked the Send Me A Status Report When This Task Is Complete option, you'll get a "Task Completed" message in your Inbox when the owner marks the task as completed.

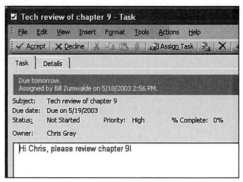

**Figure 9.13** A Task request message received by the task owner (this task request resulted from sending the form shown in Figure 9.12).

## ✔ Tips

■ Clicking the Cancel Assignment button in the Task form for an assigned task converts the task to a personal task.

■ Assigning a task won't work if you or the intended owner uses an email service that doesn't transmit the required information, such as CompuServe.

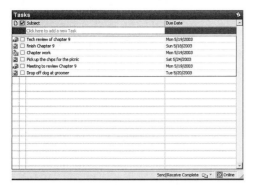

**Figure 9.14** The Tasks folder in the commonly used Simple List table review.

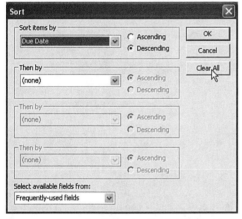

**Figure 9.15** Removing all sorting by clicking the Clear All button in the Sort dialog box.

**Figure 9.16** Adding a new task.

*This box indicates that the task was completed*

**Figure 9.17** A completed task.

# Working with Items in the Tasks Folder

You can work with the tasks in your Tasks folder in a table or in a timeline. A timeline view arranges the tasks according to their due dates, along a horizontal timeline.

## To work with your tasks in a table:

1. Open the Tasks folder and switch to any of the standard views except Task Timeline (**Figure 9.14**).

2. To sort the tasks, use the sorting techniques in Chapter 3's "To sort items" section.

3. To arrange the tasks in any order you wish (that is, not sorted by a particular field), first clear all sorting and then drag each task up or down in the list to the position where you want it.

   To clear all sorting, choose View > Arrange By > Current View > Customize Current View, click the Sort button, and then click the Clear All button (**Figure 9.15**).

4. To quickly create a new task, click in the Click Here to Add a New Task box at the top of the task list (**Figure 9.16**) and enter information into the fields shown in the view. (To enter additional information, you'll have to open the task.)

5. To quickly modify any of the task information displayed in the table, click the field and then type or select a new value.

   To designate a task as completed in the Simple List view, check the box in the second column (**Figure 9.17**).

## ✔ Tip

- To add new tasks and to modify existing ones in a particular table view, the Allow In-cell Editing and Show "New Item" row options must be checked. To access these options, choose View > Arrange By > Current View > Customize Current View and click the Other Settings button.

## To work with your tasks in a timeline:

1. Open the Tasks folder, and switch to the standard Task Timeline view (**Figure 9.18**).

2. To adjust the amount of detail shown in the timeline, click the Day, Week, or Month button on the Standard toolbar.

3. To view a particular period of time, scroll using the horizontal scroll bar.

   *or*

   Click the header (the horizontal gray bar at the top of the Information Viewer, which displays the months), and click a date on the pop-up calendar (**Figure 9.19**).

## ✔ Tips

■ To quickly view today's date, click the Today button on the Standard toolbar, or choose Go > Today.

■ To view any date, choose Go > Go To Date, or press Ctrl+G and enter the date into the Go To Date dialog box (**Figure 9.20**).

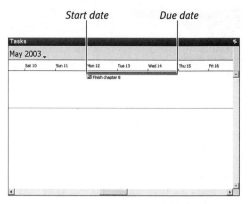

*Start date*          *Due date*

**Figure 9.18** The Tasks folder in the Task Timeline view, showing one week.

*Click anywhere in the header to display the calendar*

**Figure 9.19** Using the pop-up calendar to go to a particular date.

**Figure 9.20** The Go To Date dialog box.

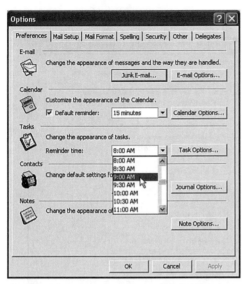

Figure 9.21 Changing the default task reminder time.

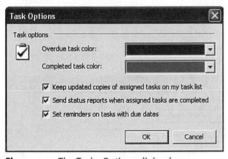

Figure 9.22 The Tasks Options dialog box.

## To set Tasks options:

◆ To change the default task reminder time, choose Tools > Options, and in the Preferences tab, type or select a time in the Reminder time list box (**Figure 9.21**).

◆ To modify the colors used for overdue and completed tasks displayed in the Outlook window, choose Tools > Options, click the Task Options button in the Preferences tab, and select new colors in the Task Options dialog box (**Figure 9.22**). To set additional default options, check each option you want Outlook to turn on by default in new tasks. (If you wish, you can turn off any of these options for a particular task.)

◆ To modify the number of hours per day or per week that Outlook uses for calculating the values you enter into the Total Work and Actual Work text boxes in the Task form, choose Tools > Options, open the Other tab, click the Advanced Options button, and type new values into the Task Working Hours per Day and Task Working Hours per Week text boxes in the Advanced Options dialog box (**Figure 9.23**). (For example, if you specify 10 hours per day, and you subsequently open the Details tab in a task and enter 20 hours into the Total work task field, Outlook will convert the value to 2 days.)

◆ To modify the features of reminders, choose Tools > Options, click the Other tab, click the Advanced Options button, and click the Reminder Options button in the Advanced Options dialog box (**Figure 9.23**).

◆ To modify features of the currently active view of the Tasks folder, choose View > Arrange By > Current View > Customize Current View, click the Other Settings button, and select the desired options in the Other Settings dialog box (for a table view) or in the Format Timeline View dialog box (for the Task Timeline view) (**Figure 9.24**).

*Enter a new value into either text box*

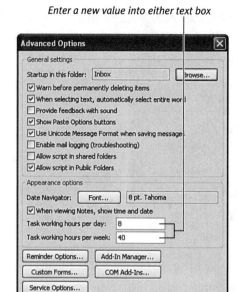

**Figure 9.23** Changing the hours per day or week that Outlook uses, in the Advanced Options dialog box.

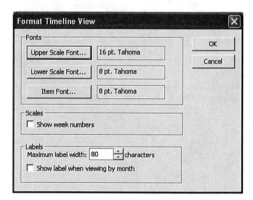

**Figure 9.24** The Format Timeline View dialog box for changing features of the Task Timeline view of the Tasks folder.

# USING THE JOURNAL

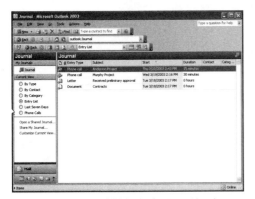

**Figure 10.1** The Journal folder in the Entry List view.

You can use the Journal folder to keep a record of various activities in your business or personal life (**Figure 10.1**). For example, you could use the Journal to record such activities as:

◆ Receiving an important email message

◆ Assigning a task to your assistant

◆ Creating a document in Word

◆ Working on an Excel worksheet

◆ Making a phone call

◆ Paying a utility bill

◆ Selling shares of a stock

In this chapter, you'll learn how to:

◆ Instruct Outlook to automatically record journal entries

◆ Create journal entries manually

◆ Work with your journal entries in a table or timeline view

◆ Open either a journal entry or the item or file that's associated with an entry

◆ Set options for the Journal folder

# Recording Journal Entries

You can create journal entries in two ways:

- You can have Outlook **automatically** record a journal entry each time a particular activity occurs that is associated with a selected contact, such as sending or receiving an email message from your editor. You can also have Outlook automatically record a journal entry each time you create or modify a document using a selected Office program, such as Microsoft Excel.

- You can **manually** create a journal entry to record any type of activity, such as making a phone call, receiving a fax, or writing a letter. When you manually create a journal entry, you can use the Journal Entry form to time the activity so that you can record its exact duration.

## ✔ Tip

- Automatic journal entries can slow operations on your computer and can consume a large amount of space in your Personal Folders file or your Exchange Server mailbox. To reduce these problems, you can minimize the number of entries Outlook automatically generates and you can frequently archive all but the most recent entries. Archiving is discussed in the section "Removing and Archiving Items" in Chapter 3," Working with Outlook Items."

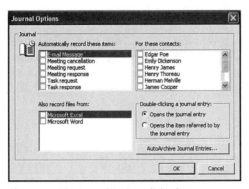

**Figure 10.2** The Journal Options dialog box.

## To record journal entries automatically:

1. Open the Journal folder.

   Outlook puts the shortcut for the Journal folder in the My Shortcuts group. If you haven't previously set up automatic journal entries, Outlook will display the Journal Options dialog box (**Figure 10.2**).

2. If Outlook doesn't automatically display the Journal Options dialog box, display it now by choosing Tools > Options and clicking the Journal Options button in the Preferences tab.

3. To have Outlook record specific activities associated with particular contacts, check the activities in the Automatically Record These Items list and check the contacts in the For These Contacts list.

   For example, if you selected E-mail Message and Task request in the first list and Edna Editor and Horatio Henning in the second, Outlook would generate a journal entry whenever you send or receive an email message or a task request to or from either of these two contacts.

4. To have Outlook create a journal entry whenever you create or modify an Office document, check the specific document types in the Also Record Files From list.

   The document types are identified by the name of the Office application that creates them. Only the applications you currently have installed will appear in the list.

5. Click the OK button.

## ✔ Tip

■ The For These Contacts list displays the contacts in your default Contacts folder only, not those in a contact-item folder you've created.

## To record journal entries manually:

1. Open the Journal folder.

2. Click the New button on the Standard toolbar, or choose Actions > New Journal Entry, or press Ctrl+N.

   *or*

   Press Ctrl+Shift+J if you are not in the Journal folder.

   Outlook will open a Journal Entry form (**Figure 10.3**).

3. Enter the desired information into the fields in the Journal Entry form:

   ▲ Type a brief description of the journal entry into the Subject text box.

   ▲ If you want to enter a full description or any other information, type it into the large text box.

   ▲ Select the type of activity you're recording in the Entry Type list box (**Figure 10.4**).

   ▲ Type the name of any company associated with the entry into the Company text box.

   ▲ Type or select the starting date and time of the activity in the Start Time list boxes.

   ▲ Type the amount of time required by the activity into the Duration list box, or select a time from the drop-down list. Alternatively, you can time an activity that's currently taking place (such as a phone call) by clicking the Start Timer button when the activity begins and clicking the Pause Timer button when the activity ends or pauses.

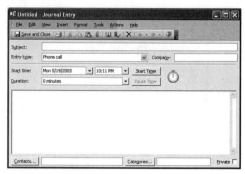

**Figure 10.3** A Journal Entry form, ready to define a new manual journal entry.

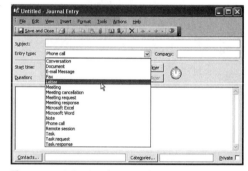

**Figure 10.4** Selecting the type of activity.

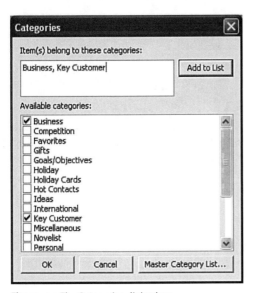

**Figure 10.5** The Categories dialos box.

▲ If a contact in your Contacts folder is associated with the journal entry (for example, the person you're calling on the phone), type the contact's name into the Contacts text box or click the Contacts button to select that contact from your Contacts folder. This will link the journal entry to the contact. You'll then be able to open the contact by double-clicking the name. Also, the Activities tab of the Contact form for that contact will list the journal entry along with any other linked Outlook items.

▲ If you want to assign a category to the journal entry, type it into the Categories text box or click the Categories button to select a category from the Categories dialog box (**Figure 10.5**). You can use a category to sort, filter, group, or find journal entries (these operations are discussed in Chapter 3).

▲ If you're sharing your Journal folder but you want the journal entry to be hidden, check the Private option. (Sharing folders is discussed in the section "Sharing Outlook Folders over a Network" in Chapter 4, "Working with Outlook Folders.")

4. Click the Save And Close toolbar button to save your new journal entry in the Journal folder and to close the form.

*continues on next page*

## ✔ Tips

- You can enter several names into the Contacts or Categories text boxes. If you type the names, separate them using commas or semicolons.

- To create journal entries manually for items not in Outlook, simply drag the item from a Windows folder to the Journal folder and modify it as you would one of the included applications.

- If you have PowerPoint, Visio, Project, or FrontPage installed, these applications appear in the Journal Options dialog box along with Word, Excel, and Access, enabling you to easily journal these additional applications.

- You can make a telephone call and record it (the event, not the actual call) in a journal entry using a single command. Open the Contacts folder, choose Actions > Call Contact > New Call or press Ctrl+Shift+D, check the Create New Journal Entry When Starting New Call option, and use the New Call dialog box to make your call (**Figure 10.6**). The use of Outlook's calling feature requires a modem to be installed on your computer, which is not covered in this book. Type in "Make a telephone call" in Microsoft Office Help for more information.

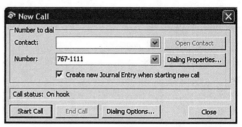

**Figure 10.6** Making a call and recording it in a journal entry.

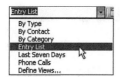

**Figure 10.7** Clicking the down arrow to select the folder view.

**Figure 10.8** Selecting the current view.

**Figure 10.9** Clicking to create a new journal entry.

# Working with Items in the Journal Folder

You can work with your journal entries either in a table or in a timeline.

When you open an item in the Journal folder, you can either open the journal entry itself in a form or open any item or document that's associated with the journal entry.

## To work with your journal entries in a table:

1. Open the Journal folder and switch to the standard Entry List, Last Seven Days, or Phone Calls view by clicking the down arrow (to the right of the View field in the Advanced Toolbar) and selecting it from the menu (**Figure 10.7**).

    *or*

    Click View > Arrange By > Current View and select it from the drop menu (**Figure 10.8**). (The Entry List view is shown in **Figure 10.1**, earlier in the chapter.)

    Entry List shows all entries, while Last Seven Days and Phone Calls apply filters to display subsets of your entries.

2. To quickly create a new journal entry, click in the Click Here to Add a New Journal Entry box at the top of the table (**Figure 10.9**) and enter information into the fields shown in the particular view. (To enter additional information, you'll have to open the journal entry in a form.)

3. To quickly modify any of the journal entry information displayed in the table, click the field and then type the change.

## ✔ Tips

- To add new journal entries and to modify existing entries in a particular table view, the Allow In-cell Editing and Show "New Item" Row options must be checked. To access these options, choose View > Arrange By > Current View > Customize Current View to display the Customize View: Entry List dialog box, and click the Other Settings button (**Figure 10.10**).

- A new journal entry defaults to the current date and time regardless of the view or dates displayed in the journal.

- Double-click on an open spot in the Journal Pane to open a new Journal Entry form.

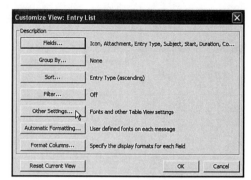

**Figure 10.10** Clicking the Other Settings button.

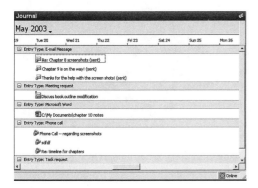

**Figure 10.11** The By Type view of the Journal folder, showing one week with all groups expanded.

*Click anywhere in the header to display the calendar*

**Figure 10.12** Using the pop-up calendar to go to a particular date.

**Figure 10.13** The Go to Date dialog box.

## To work with your journal entries in a timeline:

1. Open the Journal folder, and switch to the standard By Type, By Contact, or By Category view (**Figure 10.11**).

   Each of these views groups your journal entries using a different field. (For information on working with groups, see "To group items" in Chapter 3.)

2. To adjust the amount of detail shown in the timeline, click the Day, Week, or Month toolbar button.

3. To view a particular period of time, scroll using the horizontal scroll bar.

   *or*

   Click the header (the horizontal gray bar at the top of the Information Viewer, which displays the months), and then click a date on the pop-up calendar (**Figure 10.12**).

## ✔ Tips

- To quickly view today's date, click the Today button on the Standard toolbar, or choose Go > Today.

- To view any date, choose Go > Go to Date or press Ctrl+G, and then enter the date into the Go to Date dialog box (**Figure 10.13**).

## To open a journal entry:

◆ Double-click the entry to open the journal entry.

   *or*

   Right-click on the entry and select Open Journal Entry from the menu (**Figure 10.14**).

The entry will be opened in the Journal Entry form, where you can view and edit it.

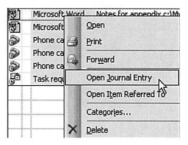

**Figure 10.14** Opening the journal entry itself.

## ✔ Tip

■ The two options mentioned in this section are explained in "To set Journal options," on the next page.

## To open the item or document associated with a journal entry:

◆ If the Opens the Item Referred to by the Journal Entry option is selected (see the tip below), double-click the entry or use any of the other methods discussed in "To open an item" in Chapter 3.

   *or*

   If the Opens the Journal Entry option is selected, right-click the entry and choose Open Item Referred To from the pop-up menu (**Figure 10.15**).

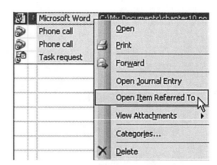

**Figure 10. 15** Opening the item or document associated with the journal entry.

An item associated with the entry will be opened in a Outlook form, and a document associated with the entry will be opened by the application used to create it (for example, a Word document will be opened in Microsoft Word).

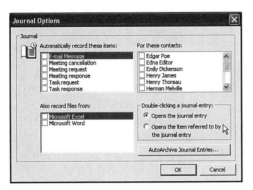

**Figure 10.16** Choosing what happens when you double-click a journal entry.

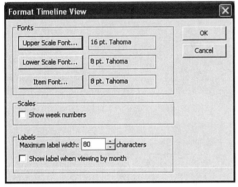

**Figure 10.17** The Format Timeline View dialog box for changing features of the By Type view of the Journal folder.

## ✔ Tips

- The two options mentioned in this section are explained in the next section, "To set Journal options."

- To open an item or document as described here, the large text box of the journal entry must contain a shortcut to the item or document. When Outlook automatically generates a journal entry, it adds the shortcut. You can also add a shortcut (or attachment, which will work as well) if you create the entry manually. See "Inserting files, items, and objects" in Chapter 3.

## To set Journal options:

- To select what happens when you double-click a journal entry (or use another method to open it), choose Tools > Options, click the Journal Options button in the Preferences tab, and select the option you want in the Journal Options dialog box (**Figure 10.16**).

  *or*

  To modify features of the currently active view of the Journal folder, choose View > Arrange By > Current View > Customize Current View, click the Other Settings button, and select the desired options in the Other Settings dialog box (for a table view) or the Format Timeline View dialog box (for a timeline view) (**Figure 10.17**).

# USING THE
# NOTES FOLDER

**Figure 11.1** The Notes folder in the Icons view, displaying large icons.

You can use the Notes folder to quickly create text notes (**Figure 11.1**). You can use notes to store information that doesn't fit into any of the other Outlook folders (for example, a shopping list). You can also quickly type information into a note that you'll later transfer to another Outlook folder. (For example, while talking on the phone, you could jot down a name and address, and then when you have more time, transfer that information to the Contacts folder.)

In this chapter, you'll learn how to:

- ◆ Create new notes

- ◆ Work with notes displayed as icons

- ◆ Work with notes in a table view

- ◆ Set options for the Notes folder

## ✔ Tip

- ■ You can use the instructions given in this chapter either with the default Notes folder or a with another note-item folder that you've created.

# Creating New Notes

Notes are the simplest of Outlook items. A note consists of a single text box, in which you can enter plain text only. You can't insert graphics or format the text in a note.

### To create a new note:

1. Open the Notes folder.

2. Click the New button on the Standard toolbar, or choose Actions > New Note, or press Ctrl+N.

   *or*

   Press Ctrl+Shift+N if you are not in the Notes folder.

   Outlook will open a blank note (**Figure 11.2**).

3. Type any text you want into the note.

   When the text you type reaches the right border of the note, Outlook automatically wraps it to the next line. To create a new line at any position in the text, press Enter.

4. To open the note's menu, click the Note icon in the upper-left corner of the note (**Figure 11.3**). To change features of the note, or to include additional information, choose appropriate commands from this menu:

   ▲ Choose a command on the Color submenu to set the background color of the note (**Figure 11.4**).

   ▲ If you want to assign one or more categories to the note, choose the Categories command to open the Categories dialog box (**Figure 11.5**). You can use a category to sort, filter, group, or find notes. (These operations are discussed in Chapter 3, "Working with Outlook Items.")

**Figure 11.2** A blank note.

*Click this icon to open the menu*

**Figure 11.3** Opening a note's menu.

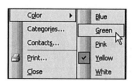

**Figure 11.4** Changing the background color of a note.

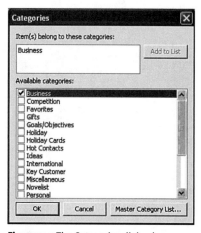

**Figure 11.5** The Categories dialog box.

**Figure 11.6** The Contacts for Note dialog box.

▲ If a contact is associated with the note, choose the Contacts command to open the Contacts for Note dialog box (**Figure 11.6**). Then type the contact's name into the text box, or click the Contacts button to select the contact from your Contacts folder. This will link the note to the contact. As a result, the Activities tab of the Contact form for that contact will list the note along with any other linked Outlook items. You can enter several contacts (if you type them, separate them using commas or semicolons).

**5.** Click the Close button in the note's upper-right corner or press Esc when you are done with the note and want to save what you have typed.

## ✔ Tips

■ Unlike in other types of Outlook forms, all changes you make in a note are saved automatically, as soon as you make them.

■ The title of the note is based on the first sentence (or line) of the note. To change the note's title, change the first line of the note.

■ You can quickly create a note in Outlook, regardless of the currently opened folder, by pressing Ctrl+Shift+N.

■ You might want to leave a note open for handy reference while you work in another Outlook folder or in another program.

CREATING NEW NOTES

# Working with Items in the Notes Folder

You can display the notes in your Notes folder either as icons or in a table.

### To work with Note icons:

1. Open the Notes folder, and switch to the Icons view.

2. To change the size of the icons, click the Large Icons, Small Icons, or List button on the Standard toolbar; or choose the equivalent commands on the View menu. These options are shown in **Figures 11.7**, **11.8**, and **11.9**.

3. To rearrange the icons (only with the Large Icons or Small Icons option), drag each icon to the position where you want it.

4. To have Outlook align the icons in rows and columns, choose View > Line Up Icons.

   *or*

   Right-click on an open area on the Notes Pane, and select Line Up Icons.

### ✔ Tip

■ Steps 3 and 4 assume that the default Do Not Arrange option is applied to the Icons view (this option is shown in **Figure 11.13**, later in the chapter).

**Figure 11.7** The Icons view showing large icons.

**Figure 11.8** The Icons view showing small icons.

**Figure 11.9** The Icons view showing an icon list.

**Figure 11.10** The Notes List view of the Notes folder.

**Figure 11.11** The Notes Options dialog box.

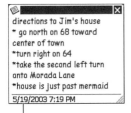

**Figure 11.12** A note showing date and time.

Date and time note was last modified

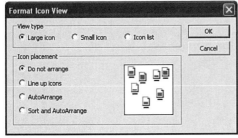

**Figure 11.13** The Format Icon View dialog box for changing features of the Icons view of the Notes folder.

## To work with notes in a table:

◆ Open the Notes folder and switch to the Notes List, Last Seven Days, By Category, or By Color view.

Notes List shows all your notes (**Figure 11.10**), Last Seven applies a filter, and By Category and By Color group your notes.

## To set Notes options:

◆ To change the note background color, size, or font, choose Tools > Options, click the Note Options button in the Preferences tab, and select options in the Notes Options dialog box (**Figure 11.11**).

The background color and note size that you select will be used as the defaults for the notes you subsequently create. (You can override either, however, for a particular note). The font you select will be applied to the text in all notes.

*or*

To hide or show the date and time at the bottom of your notes, choose Tools > Options, open the Other tab, click the Advanced Options button, and uncheck or check the When Viewing Notes, Show Time and Date option. The date and time tell you when the note was last modified (**Figure 11.12**).

*or*

To modify features of the currently active view of the Notes folder, choose View > Arrange By > Current View > Customize Current View, click the Other Settings button, and select the desired options in the Other Settings dialog box (for a Table view) or the Format Icon View dialog box (for the Icons view) (**Figure 11.13**).

# USING
# ADVANCED
# FEATURES

In this chapter, you'll learn how to accomplish some of the more advanced tasks in Outlook. Specifically, you'll learn how to:

◆ Recall and expire messages, delay sending a message, delegate folders to an assistant, and use public folders.

◆ Use the Out of Office Assistant to send automatic replies to messages when you are out of the office.

◆ Use Outlook Web Access to access your mailbox from a Web browser.

◆ Create templates and customize forms to simplify creating specific types of Outlook items.

◆ Back up and archive your Outlook items.

◆ Find specific items in your Outlook folders.

◆ Create and use Send/Receive groups, which control how and when mail accounts are processed.

## ✔ Tip

■ Several of the email topics in this chapter require Exchange Server, but many of the topics relate to all types of email accounts. Other topics relate to all types of Outlook items, not just email.

# Working with Exchange Server

Exchange Server offers some additional capabilities you won't find when working with other types of mail servers. Microsoft designed Outlook to take advantage of these additional features, which include:

◆ **You can recall a message after you send it, which deletes the message from the recipient's mailbox.** The recipient must be using Exchange Server and must not have already read the message. Use message recall when you want to "unsend" a message.

◆ **You can set a message to expire.** The message is automatically deleted if the recipient has not read it, or it is marked with strikethrough if it has been read. You can also delay delivery, which retains the message in your Outbox until the time you have specified for delivery. When the delivery time arrives, Outlook sends the message.

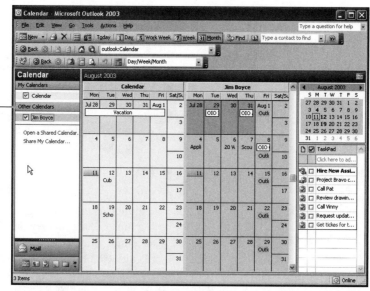

Other Calendars

**Figure 12.1** Another user's calendar open in Outlook.

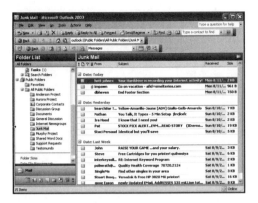

**Figure 12.2** This public folder stores junk mail.

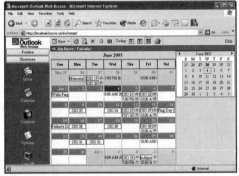

**Figure 12.3** Access a mailbox from a Web browser with Outlook Web Access.

◆ **You can delegate one or more folders to an assistant to allow that person to open the folder and work with its contents.** For example, you might delegate your Calendar folder to your secretary to manage your schedule for you. Both you and the assistant can view the schedule (**Figure 12.1**). You control whether the assistant can create or modify items, or just view the calendar.

◆ Outlook displays public folders on an Exchange Server and enables you to read messages posted to those folders and create your own posts (**Figure 12.2**). Public folders provide an easy way for Exchange Server users to share documents and discuss topics of interest.

◆ Outlook Web Access is a server-side component of Exchange Server (not part of Outlook) that enables you to access your Exchange Server mailbox from a Web browser such as Internet Explorer (**Figure 12.3**). For example, you might need to check your messages from a public kiosk or from someone else's computer when you are out of the office.

## ✔ Tip

■ See Appendix A, "Configuring Outlook," to learn how to configure an Exchange Server account.

## To recall a sent message:

1. Open Outlook and click the Sent Items folder in the Folders List, or open another folder where the sent message is stored (**Figure 12.4**).

2. Double-click the message to open it, and then choose Actions > Recall This Message to open the Recall This Message dialog box (**Figure 12.5**).

3. Choose the option Delete Unread Copies of This Message, if you simply want to delete the message from the recipient's mailbox.

   *or*

   Choose the option Delete Unread Copies and Replace with a New Message, if you want to send a replacement message.

   When you click OK, Outlook opens the message so you can edit it (**Figure 12.6**) prior to sending the replacement message. When you click Send, Outlook attempts to recall the message from the recipient's mailbox and sends the replacement.

## ✔ Tips

- You can choose the option Tell Me if Recall Succeeds or Fails for each recipient to have Outlook send you a notification message of the success or failure of the recall attempt.

- Outlook attempts to recall the message from all recipients to whom it was sent.

- Messages are recalled only if they have not already been read by the recipient. Therefore, it's possible that a message could be recalled from some recipients but not from others.

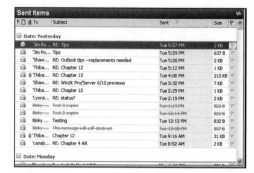

**Figure 12.4** Open the Sent Items folder.

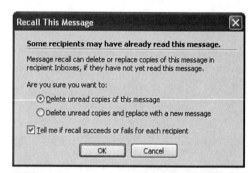

**Figure 12.5** The Recall This Message dialog box.

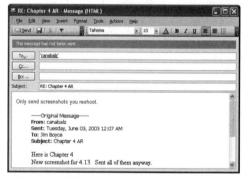

**Figure 12.6** Edit the message and resend it.

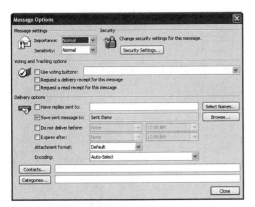

**Figure 12.7** The Message Options dialog box.

Select a date     Select a time

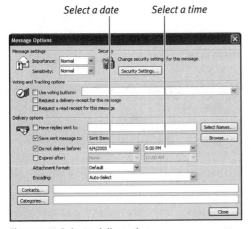

**Figure 12.8** Select a delivery time.

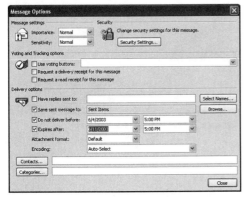

**Figure 12.9** Select a message expiration time.

## To set a message to expire or delay delivery:

1. Open Outlook and compose a new message (or open a message for forwarding or reply).

2. Choose View > Options to open the Message Options dialog box (**Figure 12.7**).

3. Select the option Do Not Deliver Before if you want to delay sending, and then select a date and time from the corresponding drop-down lists (**Figure 12.8**).

4. To set an expiration date and time for the message, select the option Expires After, and then select a date and time from the corresponding drop-down lists (**Figure 12.9**).

5. Click Close to close the Message Options dialog box, and then click Send to send the message.

## ✔ Tips

■ The capability to expire or delay messages are not tied to one another. You can choose either or both options for a particular message, as needed.

■ Use the message expiration feature when you want a message to be available to a recipient for a very specific period of time. Exchange Server removes the message from the recipient's Inbox when the expiration time arrives if the message has not been read. If the message has been read, Exchange Server marks the message header with strikethrough to indicate that the message has expired.

■ Use the delayed delivery option when you want to compose a message and place it in the Outbox but not send it until a specific date and time.

## To delegate folders to an assistant:

1. Open Outlook, and choose Tools > Options; then click the Delegates tab (**Figure 12.10**) in the Options dialog box. This tab appears only if you are using Exchange Server.

2. Click Add to open the Add Users dialog box (**Figure 12.11**).

3. Select a person from the address list, click Add, and then click OK.

   Outlook opens the Delegate Permissions dialog box (**Figure 12.12**).

4. For each folder you want to delegate, select the desired permission level from the folder's drop-down list.

   The permission level determines the actions the delegate can take with the folder and its contents.

5. To have Outlook send a message to the delegate explaining the permissions they have in the folder(s), choose the option Automatically Send a Message to Delegate Summarizing These Permissions.

6. If you want the delegate to be able to see items that you have marked private, select the option Delegate Can See My Private Items.

   This setting applies to all folders for which the delegate has at least Reviewer permission.

7. Click OK, and then click OK again to close the Options dialog box.

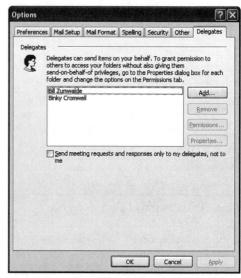

**Figure 12.10** The Delegates tab.

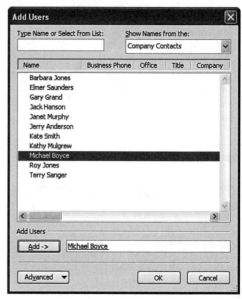

**Figure 12.11** The Add Users dialog box.

WORKING WITH EXCHANGE SERVER

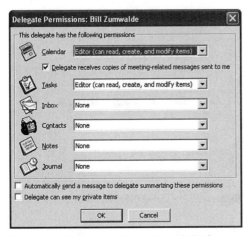

**Figure 12.12** The Delegate Permissions dialog box.

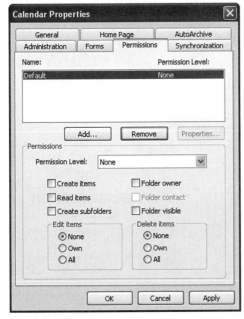

**Figure 12.13** A folder's Permissions tab.

## ✔ Tips

- You can add more than one delegate to a folder, and also set their permissions differently to give them different levels of access to the folder.

- You can fine-tune permissions to grant or remove certain capabilities, such as the capability for a delegate to create subfolders. To modify permissions, open the folder list, right-click the folder, and choose Properties. Use the Permissions tab (**Figure 12.13**) to modify permissions in this way.

- You can also modify permissions for a specific delegate with the Options dialog box. Choose Tools > Options, click the Delegate tab, select a delegate, and click Permissions to open the Delegate Permissions dialog box, previously shown in **Figure 12.12**.

- Make sure to leave unchecked the option Delegate Can See My Private Items if you don't want your delegate to be able to view your private items.

- The Appointment tab of the Appointment form, the Task tab of the Task form, and the Journal Entry form include a Private check box you can use to mark an item as private. To mark a contact as private, open the contact, click the All Fields tab, select All Contact Fields from the Select From drop-down list, and change to Yes the value of the Private field in the resulting field list.

## To modify delegate permissions:

1. Open the folder list, right-click the folder, choose Properties, and then click the Permissions tab (**Figure 12.13**).

2. Select the delegate whose permissions you want to change, or select Default from the name list if you want to change default permissions.

3. Place a check mark beside each permission you want to grant to the delegate. For example, you might grant a delegate the permission to create subfolders in the selected folder.

4. In the Edit Items and Delete Items groups, select the items that you want the delegate to be able to modify and delete, respectively, and then click OK to close the dialog box.

## To use the Out of Office Assistant:

1. In Outlook, open your Inbox and choose Tools > Out of Office Assistant to open the Out of Office Assistant dialog box (**Figure 12.14**).

2. In the AutoReply text box, enter the reply message you want sent when you receive a message while your status is set to out-of-office.

3. Select I Am Currently Out of the Office and click OK.

**Figure 12.14** The Out of Office Assistant dialog box.

## ✔ Tips

- The Out of Office Assistant works as a server-side rule, so Outlook does not have to be running to process the automatic replies.

- Exchange Server sends an automatic reply only once to each sender; subsequent messages from a sender do not trigger an automatic reply. When you set your status back to In the Office, Exchange Server resets the sender list. The next time you set status to Out of the Office, Exchange Server will send an automatic reply to all senders for their first message.

- You can click Add Rule in the Out of Office Assistant dialog box to create a rule to respond with a special message for certain senders, create exceptions to the automatic replies, or take other actions.

**WORKING WITH EXCHANGE SERVER**

## To use public folders:

1. Open Outlook, open the folder list, and then expand the Public Folders branch. Expand All Public Folders (**Figure 12.15**).

2. Click on the public folder in which you want to read or post messages.

3. In the right pane (**Figure 12.16**), double-click a message to open it and read the message's contents (**Figure 12.17**).

4. Click Post Reply to open a reply form (**Figure 12.18**), type a subject and message, and click Save to save the message to the folder.

### ✔ Tips

- Choose View > Arrange By > Conversation to sort the messages by conversation topic.

- The Exchange Server administrator determines the permissions you have in a public folder, which determines whether you can read, post, or delete messages (or a combination thereof) in the folder.

**Figure 12.16** Posted messages in a public folder.

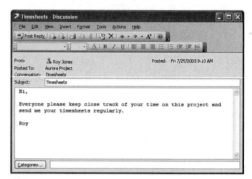

**Figure 12.17** Reading a posted message.

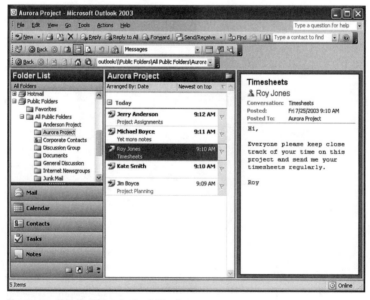

**Figure 12.15** Public folders in the folder list.

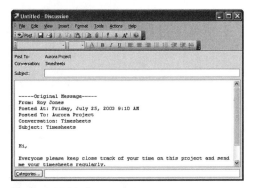

**Figure 12.18** Posting a reply to a message.

**Figure 12.19** Logging on to Outlook Web Access.

*You can select a different folder here* — *Your Inbox*

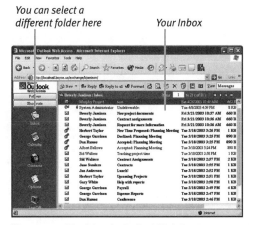

**Figure 12.20** The Inbox in Outlook Web Access.

## To access your mailbox from a Web browser:

1. Open Internet Explorer or other Web browser, and enter the address **http://*server*/exchange**, where *server* is the name or IP address of your Exchange Server, or the Web site under which Outlook Web Access is hosted.

   For example, a valid address might be http://webmail.boyce.us/exchange.

2. Outlook Web Access prompts you to log on to the Exchange Server (**Figure 12.19**). Enter your Exchange Server account name and password, and click OK.

3. Your Inbox appears in your Web browser (**Figure 12.20**), much as it does in Outlook. Double-click a message to open and read it, or click a different folder in the left frame (which is similar to the Navigation pane in Outlook) to work with other folders.

4. Use the buttons just above the message header list to move forward and backward through the list of messages in your Inbox.

## ✔ Tips

- Your administrator determines the address for Outlook Web Access to your Exchange Server. Check with your Exchange Server administrator to determine the correct address to use.

- If entering your user name and password does not allow you to connect to Outlook Web Access, enter your username in the format <domain>\<user>, where <domain> is the domain where your account resides, and <user> is your account name.

- The Outlook Web Access interface is similar enough to Outlook that you should not have any problems learning to use Outlook Web Access once you have some experience using Outlook.

# Using Templates for Repetitive Tasks

Although it sometimes seems like computers make your work more difficult, most of the time they make it easier. One area where computers really shine is in repetitive tasks. For example, you might need to send the same message frequently to one or more people. Or, maybe you need to add several people to your Contacts folder, and all of them work for the same company and therefore have the same address or even phone number.

A template in Outlook is an Outlook item that you save by name to disk. For example, you might create a standard message and save it as a template. You can then open the template, make changes as needed, and send the message on its way. Templates, therefore, save you the time required to re-create repetitive information.

◆ You can save any type of Outlook item, except a note, as a template. You must specify a name and location for the template when you save it, and use this name and location to later open the template when needed.

◆ Templates are useful in conjunction with rules. You might create an email template with a standard reply, and then create a rule that sends that template as the reply to incoming messages that fit certain conditions, such as specific text in the subject.

◆ When you create a template, enter all of the information that will remain the same each time you use the template. Add other information as needed when you create a new item from the template. You can also change existing information in the template when you create an item from it.

**Figure 12.21** The Save As dialog box.

**Figure 12.22** The Choose Form dialog box.

**Figure 12.23** Selecting a template to open.

## To create a template:

1. Start a new item, such as a mail message or appointment.

2. Enter information in the item's form as needed, such as subject, body text, recipient addresses, or other information.

3. Choose File, Save As to open the Save As dialog box (**Figure 12.21**).

4. From the Save As Type drop-down list, choose Outlook Template.

5. In the File Name field, enter a name for the template that will help you identify the template's purpose when you need to locate it again.

6. From the Save In drop-down list, choose the location in which to save the template. Choose the default Templates folder to make it easy to locate the template later.

7. Click Save to save the template and close the Save As dialog box.

8. When you need to use the form, choose Tools > Forms > Choose a Form to open the Choose Form dialog box (**Figure 12.22**).

9. From the Look In drop-down list, choose User Templates in File System and then select a template (**Figure 12.23**). Click Open to open the template.
   Outlook opens the item's form.

10. Complete the item, and click Send or Save and Close, depending on the item type.

*continues on next page*

## ✔ Tips

- You can share templates with others by placing them on a network server. To open a template from a network server, choose User Templates in File System in the Choose Form dialog box, and then click Browse to browse to the server.

- If you need to change a template's contents, open the template, make the changes, then choose File > Save As, select the existing name, and click Save. Click Yes when prompted to overwrite the existing template.

- You can customize the forms Outlook uses for each item type, as well as create your own custom forms for other purposes. Creating custom forms is a higher level topic not covered in this book. To get started, choose Tools > Forms > Design a Form.

*Archive folders*

**Figure 12.24** The Archive folders appear in the folder list.

# Archiving Outlook Items

Many people who use Outlook come to rely on it heavily to store their contacts, messages, appointments, and other important day-to-day information. For that reason, it's important that you back up your Outlook data in the event your computer crashes, or you lose your mail or other items for some other reason.

In addition to backing up items, you can use Outlook's AutoArchive feature to automatically move old items to a set of archive folders. Moving these items to your archive folders removes them from your mail store (such as Personal Folders) to reduce clutter and improve performance, but keeps them available in case you need them in the future.

Some important points to remember about archiving Outlook items are:

◆ Archived items are stored in a Personal Folder (PST) file. You can move the file from one computer to another, if needed.

◆ You can archive items manually as needed or set up each folder to automatically archive items that fit the age you specify. You specify global AutoArchive settings, but you can also specify overriding settings for each folder.

◆ By default, Outlook includes the Archive folders in the folder list (**Figure 12.24**). You can configure Outlook to remove the Archive folders from your folder list, and then simply choose File > Open > Outlook Data File whenever you need to work with it.

*continues on next page*

**ARCHIVING OUTLOOK ITEMS**

## ✔ Tips

- If you have an Exchange Server account, your Exchange Server administrator probably makes backup copies of your mailbox. You can still use the AutoArchive feature to make an additional copy of your old items or export important items to a different set of folders for safekeeping. It's often easier for you to recover an item from your archive than to have the administrator recover it from a server-side backup.

- Periodically copy your Archive and backup PST files to a recordable CD, a network server, or local hard disk other than the one on which they are normally stored. You can use this backup in case your hard disk crashes and your archive or backup PSTs are lost.

### To back up one or more folders:

1. Open Outlook and choose File > Import and Export to open the Import and Export Wizard (**Figure 12.25**).

2. Choose Export to a File, and click Next.

3. Choose Personal Folder File (.pst), and click Next to open the Export Personal Folders dialog box (**Figure 12.26**).

4. Select the folder you want to export, or select the upper-most item (Personal Folders or Mailbox) to back up your entire Outlook store. Choose Include Subfolders to back up everything under the selected folder.

5. If you want to back up only selected items, click Filter to open the Filter dialog box (**Figure 12.27**).

   Specify conditions that identify the items you want to back up (such as all messages from a specific sender or with a specific subject, received within the past two weeks, and so on).

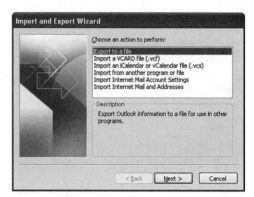

**Figure 12.25** The Import and Export Wizard.

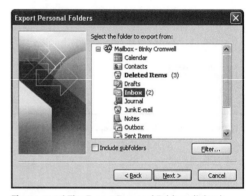

**Figure 12.26** The Export Personal Folders dialog box.

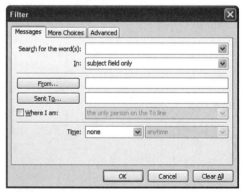

**Figure 12.27** The Filter dialog box.

*Choose how to treat duplicate items in your personal folders*

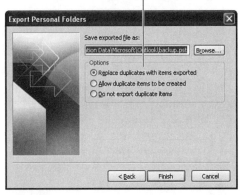

**Figure 12.28** The Export Personal Folders dialog box.

**6.** Click OK when you're satisfied with the filter settings, and then click Next to display the Export Personal Folders dialog box (**Figure 12.28**).

**7.** In the Save Export File As field, enter the path and filename for the backup file. Click Browse to browse for a location, if needed.

**8.** Choose how you want Outlook to treat duplicate items if an item already exists in the target PST, and then click Finish.

## ✔ Tips

■ Make sure to choose the Include Subfolders option to back up everything in a folder, including other folders. This is particularly important if you are backing up your entire mailbox or whole set of Personal Folders.

■ The wizard defaults to using a path and filename within your Windows user profile. You can specify a different location, such as My Documents, if you frequently need to open the backup file to retrieve items.

## To set global AutoArchive options:

1. In Outlook, choose Tools > Options, click the Other tab, and click AutoArchive to open the AutoArchive dialog box (**Figure 12.29**).

2. Specify the desired frequency for AutoArchive with the option Run AutoArchive Every *n* Days, and then select the number of days from the spin control.

3. In the During AutoArchive area, set options using the following list as a guide:

   ▲ **Delete Expired Items**. Have AutoArchive delete email messages that have expired. (See "To set a message to expire or delay delivery" earlier in this chapter for more details on message expiration.)

   ▲ **Archive or Delete Old Items**. Have Outlook archive or delete items that meet the AutoArchive age criteria you specify with the Clean Out Items Older Than option.

   ▲ **Show Archive Folder in Folder List**. Choose this option to include the Archive PST in the folder list for easy access to archived items.

   ▲ **Clean Out Items Older Than**. Specify the aging period for items that you want archived.

   ▲ **Move Old Items To**. Choose this option to move archive items to a PST file and specify the path and filename.

   ▲ **Permanently Delete Old Items**. Choose this option if you want items to be deleted instead of archived to a PST.

**Figure 12.29** The AutoArchive dialog box.

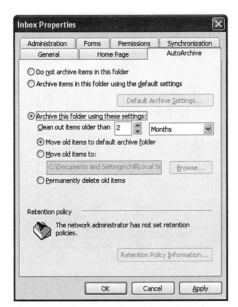

**Figure 12.30** The AutoArchive tab of a folder's properties.

✔ **Tips**

■ You can enable archiving for some folders and leave it off for others. For example, you probably don't need to archive the Deleted Items folder, or folders you never use.

■ Archiving is not enabled by default for individual folders, even if you enable it in the global AutoArchive options. You must explicitly enable AutoArchive for a particular folder to have its contents archived automatically.

✔ **Tips**

■ The global AutoArchive options apply to all folders that do not have explicit AutoArchive settings of their own, and which are configured to AutoArchive (see the following section).

■ Setting global AutoArchive options is just the first step. You must also configure AutoArchive options for each folder to include them in AutoArchive.

■ Enable the option Prompt before AutoArchive Runs if you want Outlook to warn you before it archives items (and gives you the option to cancel the archive).

## To set AutoArchive options for a single folder:

1. Open Outlook, open the folder list, right-click a folder, and choose Properties. Then, click the AutoArchive tab (**Figure 12.30**).

2. Choose Archive Items in This Folder Using the Default Settings if you want AutoArchive to archive the folder using the global settings.

   Choose Archive This Folder Using These Settings if you want to specify unique AutoArchive settings for the folder.

3. Set options for the folder as desired. These settings are essentially the same as the global settings described previously.

4. Click OK to close the dialog box, and then repeat the process for other folders that you want Outlook to automatically archive.

## To manually archive folders:

1. Open Outlook, open the folder list, and click a folder.

2. Choose File > Archive to open the Archive dialog box (**Figure 12.31**).

3. To archive all folders that have AutoArchive enabled, choose the option Archive All Folders According to Their AutoArchive Settings.

   To archive only the selected folder and its subfolders, choose the option Archive This Folder and All Subfolders.

4. Select a date from the drop-down list to specify the age of items to be archived.

5. Select the option Include Items With "Do Not AutoArchive" Checked to also archive items that are marked to be excluded from archiving.

6. Accept the default archive file or specify a different one in the Archive file field, and then click OK to archive the items.

## ✔ Tips

■ To mark an item to be excluded from archiving, open the item and choose File > Properties. Place a check in the Do Not AutoArchive This Item check box, and then click OK. Clear this check box if you later decide you want the item to be archived.

■ If you configure a folder to permanently delete old items during AutoArchive, those items are removed permanently; they are not placed in the Deleted Items folder.

**Figure 12.31** The Archive dialog box.

# Using Send/Receive Groups

If you use more than one email account and don't want to check all of them at the same time, you can create and use *Send/Receive groups* to control how and when Outlook checks for messages. A Send/Receive group is a named group of account settings that define which accounts are checked and how Outlook downloads waiting mail from each.

Following are some key points to understand about Send/Receive groups:

◆ Outlook creates a default group named All Accounts and by default includes all email accounts in that group when performing a Send/Receive with the group.

◆ Unless you configure a group to be excluded, Outlook processes all Send/Receive groups when you press F9, click Send/Receive on the toolbar, or choose Tools > Send/Receive > Send/Receive All.

◆ You can selectively process a single group, when needed, by choosing Tools > Send/Receive and clicking *group*, where *group* is the name of the Send/Receive group to process.

## ✔ Tips

■ A Send/Receive group not only specifies which accounts to process but whether to send mail, receive mail, or both; which folders should by synchronized; whether to download entire messages and attachments or just message headers; and for POP3 and Exchange Server accounts, only download headers for messages larger than a size you specify.

■ You can create and use more than one Send/Receive group. For example, you might create a group to check your business-related messages and another to check your personal messages. Or, perhaps you would create a group to check your Exchange Server and POP3 accounts, and create another group to check your Hotmail account.

## To create or change a Send/Receive group:

1. Choose Tools > Send/Receive > Send/ Receive Settings > Define Send/Receive Groups to open the Send/Receive Groups dialog box (**Figure 12.32**).

2. Click New to open the Send/Receive Group Name dialog box, type a name for the group, and click OK.

   *or*

   Click an existing group, and click Edit to open the Send/Receive Settings dialog box for the group (**Figure 12.33**).

3. Click an account in the Accounts list at the left, and then select the option Include the Selected Account in This Group to have Outlook include the account when processing the selected group.

4. For all accounts, choose Send Mail Items if you want to send outgoing mail waiting in an account's Outbox.

   For Exchange Server and POP3 accounts, choose Receive Mail Items to retrieve waiting mail on the server.

   For an IMAP account, choose Get Unread Folder Count if you want Outlook to check the number of waiting unread messages on the IMAP server.

5. In the Folder Options area, place a check beside the folder(s) you want synchronized with the server when Outlook processes the Send/Receive group.

6. For all accounts, choose Download Headers Only if you want Outlook to download only message headers without the message body or attachment. You can then mark the messages for download or deletion, as desired.

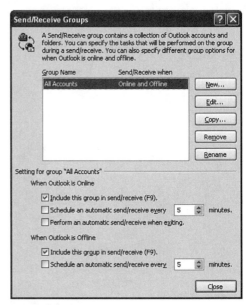

**Figure 12.32** The Send/Receive Groups dialog box.

**Figure 12.33** A group's Send/Receive Settings dialog box.

For Exchange Server and POP3 accounts, choose Download Complete Item Including Attachment to download the entire message. Optionally, select Download Only Headers for Items Larger Than, and then specify a size limit. Outlook downloads the entire item only if it is smaller than the specified size.

7. After you have configured all accounts in the group as needed, click OK.

8. In the Send/Receive Groups dialog box, select a group and select the Include This Group in Send/Receive option if you want Outlook to process the group when you click Send/Receive on the toolbar; or press F9. Clear this check box if you don't want Outlook to process the group.

   Repeat this step for each group, and then click OK.

## ✔ Tips

■ Enable the option Schedule an Automatic Send/Receive Every $n$ Minutes if you want Outlook to automatically send/receive messages at the interval specified. There are two settings for this: one for when Outlook is online and another for when it is offline.

■ Enable the option Perform an Automatic Send/Receive when exiting to have Outlook send/receive when you exit the program.

USING SEND/RECEIVE GROUPS

## To process a specific account or group:

1. To send/receive for a single account, choose Tools > Send/Receive > *account* Only, where *account* is the account name (**Figure 12.34**). Then click Inbox.

2. To send/receive for all accounts in a Send/Receive group, choose Tools > Send/Receive > *group*, where *group* is the Send/Receive group name (**Figure 12.35**).

## ✔ Tip

■ Check the settings for each Send/Receive group to make sure you don't have it configured to be checked when performing a send/receive, unless you want that group to be processed.

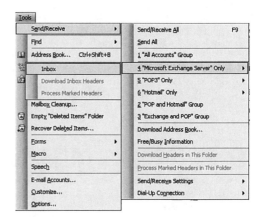

**Figure 12.34** Processing a single account.

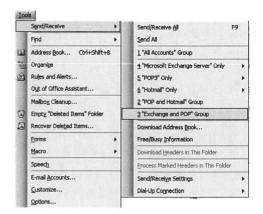

**Figure 12.35** Processing a group of accounts.

# EXPLORING THE WEB IN OUTLOOK

You can use Outlook as a tool for exploring the Web. You can view Web pages within the Outlook window, or you can use Outlook to open pages in your default Web browser program (for example, Microsoft Internet Explorer or Netscape Navigator).

In this chapter, you'll learn how to:

◆ Add the Favorites menu to Outlook to quickly access frequently used Web pages

◆ Display a Web page in the Outlook window by using the Favorites menu, and how to add a Web page to this menu

◆ Display a Web page in your browser by opening an Internet shortcut file

◆ Use the Web toolbar to open and navigate through Web pages

◆ Create a shortcut to a Web page in the Navigation pane so that you can display the page in the Outlook window by simply clicking the shortcut

◆ Attach a home page to an Outlook folder so that you can display Web-style information in that folder in addition to the folder's contents

# Displaying a Web Page

When you open a Web page using Outlook, the page will be displayed within the Outlook window (**Figure 13.1**) in your Web browser (**Figure 13.2**), depending on which of the methods in this chapter that you use.

Once you've opened a Web page, you can view other pages by clicking any hyperlinks that are displayed within the original page.

Outlook does not by default include the Favorites menu, which lists your favorite Web sites. However, you can easily add this menu—which is available in the Start menu and Internet Explorer—to Outlook to make it easier to access your favorite Web sites from Outlook.

You can also add Internet shortcuts on the desktop, and then move them to Outlook to make them accessible from Outlook.

## ✔ Tips

- If you are using another Web browser, such as Netscape or Opera, you can copy your favorites to the Windows Favorites folder to make them available to Outlook.

- If you click a Web-page hyperlink inserted in an Outlook item, the page will be opened in your browser. See "To edit a new or existing item" and **Figure 3.18** in Chapter 3, "Working with Outlook Items."

- You can open a contact's Web page in your browser by selecting the contact in the Outlook window and clicking the Explore Web Page button on the Advanced toolbar, or by pressing Ctrl+Shift+X. See "To contact a contact" in Chapter 8, "Using the Contacts Folder."

**Figure 13.1** Outlook can open a Web page right in Outlook.

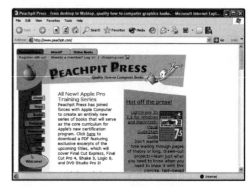

**Figure 13.2** Some pages open in your default Web browser.

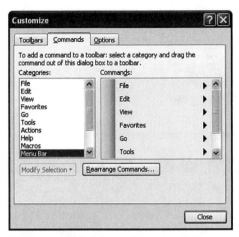

**Figure 13.3** Add Favorites to the menu with the Customize dialog box.

*First, click Menu Bar...*   *...then, click Favorites and drag to the menu bar*

**Figure 13.4** Drag Favorites onto the menu bar.

■ You can attach a Web page to an Outlook folder and display it rather than the folder's normal contents. See "Attaching a Home Page to an Outlook Folder" later in this chapter.

## To add the Favorites menu to Outlook:

1. Right-click the menu bar and choose Customize.

2. Click the Commands tab (**Figure 13.3**) and scroll through the Categories list to locate Menu Bar.

3. Click Menu Bar in the Categories list, and then click on Favorites in the Commands list (**Figure 13.4**) and drag it to the desired location on the menu bar (such as between the View and Go menus).

4. Click Close in the Customize dialog box.

## ✔ Tips

■ The & character causes Outlook to underline the F in Favorites, making it a shortcut key for the Favorites menu.

■ You do not have to place the Favorites menu on the menu bar itself. Instead, you can drop the Favorites menu on another Outlook menu, such as the View menu, to reduce the number of menus listed in the menu bar.

■ You can customize the menu bar to add or remove commands as you see fit. See Chapter 14, "Customizing Outlook," for details on customizing toolbars and menu bars.

■ If you decide to reset the menu bar back to its default state, right-click the menu bar and choose Customize. Click the Toolbars tab, click Menu Bar in the list, click Reset, and then click OK.

**DISPLAYING A WEB PAGE**

### To open a Web page using the Favorites menu:

◆ Choose the name of the page you want to open from the Favorites menu or from one of its submenus (**Figure 13.5**).

Outlook will display the page within the Outlook window.

### ✔ Tips

■ The Web pages displayed on your Favorites menu correspond to the Internet shortcuts that are stored in the Favorites file folder of your user profile, typically stored in \Documents and Settings\*user*\Favorites, where *user* is your logon account name.

■ You can add an Internet shortcut to your Favorites file folder, thereby adding the Web page to your Favorites menu, by opening the page in Outlook, choosing Favorites > Add To Favorites, and specifying a name and location for the shortcut in the Add To Favorites dialog box (**Figure 13.6**).

### To open a Web page using an Internet shortcut:

1. Open the file folder that contains the Internet shortcut to the Web page you want to view.

   To open a file folder, click its shortcut in the Navigation Pane or use any of the other methods given in the sections "To open a file folder" and "Other ways to open folders" in Chapter 2, "Getting Started Using Outlook."

2. Double-click the Internet shortcut.

   An Internet shortcut has an icon that displays an arrow and a symbol for Internet Explorer (**Figure 13.7**).

   The Web page will be opened in your default Web browser.

**Figure 13.5** Open a page from the Favorites menu.

*First, click Favorites shortcut...*

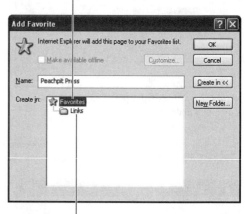

*...then, double-click the Links folder*

**Figure 13.6** Add pages to Favorites with the Add Favorite dialog box.

*Internet shortcut*

**Figure 13.7** Shortcuts to Web pages in the Favorites folder.

**DISPLAYING A WEB PAGE**

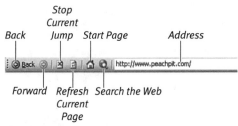

*Stop*
*Current*
*Back    Jump    Start Page              Address*

*Forward    Refresh    Search the Web*
*Current*
*Page*

**Figure 13.8** Surf the Internet with the Web toolbar.

**Figure 13.9** Choose a previously typed address.

**Figure 13.10** The Create Shortcut Wizard.

**Figure 13.11** Enter a name for the shortcut.

## To use the Web toolbar:

1. If the Web toolbar (**Figure 13.8**) isn't already displayed, choose View > Toolbars > Web.

2. To open a particular Web page in the Outlook window, type the Internet address into the Address list box on the Web toolbar.

   *or*

   Select a previously typed address from the drop-down list of the Address list box (**Figure 13.9**).

3. To navigate through the Web pages you've viewed in the Outlook window, click the Back or Forward button on the Web toolbar.

4. To stop loading the current page (for example, if your Internet connection has bogged down and loading is taking too long), click the Stop button.

5. To reload the current page, click the Refresh button.

## To create a shortcut on the desktop to a Web page:

1. Right-click the desktop, and choose New > Shortcut.

2. In the Create Shortcut Wizard (**Figure 13.10**), type the URL to the page, such as http://www.peachpit.com, and then click Next.

3. Type a name for the shortcut (**Figure 13.11**), and click Finish.

## To create a shortcut to a Web page in your Navigation pane:

1. If the shortcut is not listed in your Favorites folder, create a shortcut on the desktop to the page as explained in the previous task.

2. If the page is listed in Favorites, open My Computer, open Drive C:, and then open \Documents and Settings\*user*\Favorites, where *user* is your logon account name.

   *or*

   If you created a shortcut on the desktop, restore Outlook to a window and move it so you can see the Navigation pane and the shortcut on the desktop.

3. In the Navigation pane, open the shortcut group where you want to add the new shortcut.

4. Drag the shortcut's icon from the Favorites folder or the desktop (or other location, if applicable) to the Navigation pane. Drop it on the name of the shortcut group where you want it placed (**Figure 13.12**).

5. If you want to rename the shortcut, right-click it and choose Rename Shortcut from the pop-up menu.

   You can click the new shortcut to quickly open the Web page and display it in the Outlook window.

## ✔ Tip

■ For information on creating and managing Navigation pane shortcuts and shortcut groups, see "Modifying the Navigation Pane" in Chapter 14.

*Drag the shortcut icon...*      *...to the shortcut group in the Navigation pane*

**Figure 13.12** Drag a shortcut to a shortcut group.

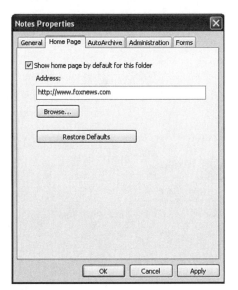

**Figure 13.13** Enter a folder home page on the Home Page tab.

# Attaching a Home Page to an Outlook Folder

As explained in Chapter 5, "Using Outlook Today," the Outlook Today folder has a home page that is displayed by default whenever the folder is opened. You can also assign a home page to any other Outlook folder, such as Inbox or Calendar. You can use a home page to display any information you want— for example, instructions for working with the folder. You can have the page displayed automatically when the folder is opened or have it displayed through a command.

### To assign a home page to an Outlook folder:

1. Open the Outlook folder.

2. Choose File > Folder > Properties For "Folder Name," where "Folder Name" is the name of the opened folder.

3. Open the Home Page tab in the Properties dialog box (**Figure 13.13**).

4. Type the full file path of the Web-page file you want to use into the Address text box (for example, C:\My Documents\ CalendarInfo.htm).

   *or*

   Click the Browse button and select the Web-page file on a local or network disk.

   *or*

   If the page is located on the Web, type its full Internet address (for example, http://www.boyce.us/).

5. Check Show Home Page by Default for This Folder.

   If you don't check this option, the normal folder contents will be displayed when you open the folder.

6. Click the OK button in the Properties dialog box.

*continues on next page*

## ✔ Tips

- The home page you assign to a folder must be contained in a Web-page (HTML) file. You can use an existing HTML file on a local or network disk or on the Web. Or, you can create an HTML file using Microsoft Word, Microsoft FrontPage, or another Web-page designer.

- You can view a folder home page only if the Show Home Page by Default for This Folder option is selected for the folder. Otherwise, the normal folder view is displayed.

- Keep in mind that if the home page is on the Web and if you have a dial-up Internet connection, Outlook will have to dial your service provider each time it displays the page.

# CUSTOMIZING OUTLOOK

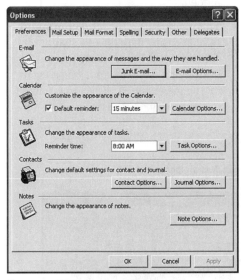

**Figure 14.1** The Preferences tab.

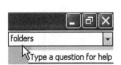

**Figure 14.2**
Enter new search text.

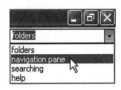

**Figure 14.3**
Select recently searched keywords.

In this chapter, you'll learn some of the useful ways that you can customize Outlook. Specifically, you'll learn how to:

◆ Customize the Outlook toolbars and menus to suit your working style

◆ Change the Office Assistant to make it look and behave the way you want

◆ Modify the Navigation Pane to organize your information and make it easier to access your folders

◆ Adjust Outlook views to enhance the way Outlook displays information

## ✔ Tips

■ You can modify many features of Outlook by choosing Tools > Options and changing settings in the Options dialog box (**Figure 14.1**). Most of these settings are discussed in this book.

■ You can obtain help on any setting by clicking the Help button near the upper-right corner of the dialog box and then typing in the search criteria.

or

Type in the search criteria and hit the Return key in the Help window (**Figure 14.2**) just above the Help button. You can also click the down arrow to the right of the text box (**Figure 14.3**) to display and select from recent searches.

# Customizing the Toolbars and Menus

Like the other major Office applications, Outlook lets you extensively customize the toolbars and the menu bar. Before delving into the details, you'll need to understand a few definitions:

◆ A **built-in toolbar** is one of the toolbars supplied with the program. The built-in toolbars available in the main Outlook window are Standard, Advanced, and Web.

◆ A **custom toolbar** is one that you create yourself.

◆ The **Outlook menu bar** initially displays the main program menus: File, Edit, View, Go, Tools, Actions, and Help (**Figure 14.4**). You can use and

customize the menu bar just like a built-in toolbar. The primary difference between the menu bar and a built-in toolbar is that the menu bar can't be hidden.

◆ This chapter uses the term **command** to refer to any item on a toolbar or on the menu bar. The term includes a button or a menu on a toolbar, a menu on the menu bar, as well as a command or a submenu on a menu.

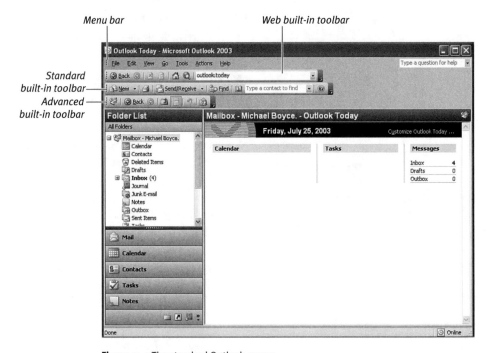

Menu bar      Web built-in toolbar

Standard built-in toolbar

Advanced built-in toolbar

**Figure 14.4** The standard Outlook screen.

*Move handle*

**Figure 14.5** Drag a toolbar to move it.

*Floating toolbar*

**Figure 14.6** Toolbars can float.

*Title bar*

**Figure 14.7** Drag a toolbar by its title bar.

## ✔ Tips

■ Instructions for using menus and toolbars are given in the section "Learning Basic Windows and Office Techniques" in Chapter 2, "Getting Started with Outlook."

■ You can use the instructions in this chapter to modify either the toolbars and menus in the main Outlook window or those in Outlook forms. To modify the toolbars and menus in the main Outlook window, activate that window before following the instructions. To modify the toolbars and menus in Outlook forms, open any form except a note before following the instructions. Modifications you make in any form (such as a Message form) will affect all other forms except a note.

## To move a toolbar or the menu bar:

◆ Drag the move handle on the toolbar or menu bar (**Figure 14.5**). If you drop the bar near an edge of the Outlook window or form, the bar will be docked (that is, positioned) along that edge. The toolbars and the menu bar in **Figures 14.4** and **14.5** are docked. If you drop the bar anywhere else on the screen, it will float at that position (**Figure 14.6**).

*or*

If the toolbar or the menu bar is floating, drag its title bar to move it (**Figure 14.7**).

## To modify a toolbar or the menu bar:

1. To modify a toolbar that isn't visible, display it by choosing View > Toolbars and then choosing the toolbar name from the submenu.

2. To display or remove standard commands from a built-in toolbar:

   If the toolbar is docked, click the down-arrow on the end of the toolbar, click Add Or Remove Buttons, choose *toolbar* where *toolbar* is the name of the toolbar selected (Standard, Advanced, or Web), and then check a command to display it or uncheck a command to remove it (**Figure 14.8**).

   *or*

   If the built-in toolbar is floating, click the down-arrow in the upper-right corner of the toolbar, click Add Or Remove Buttons, *toolbar*, and then check a command to display it or uncheck a command to remove it (**Figure 14.9**).

3. To add *any* available command to the menu bar or to a built-in or custom toolbar, choose Tools > Customize and open the Commands tab (**Figure 14.10**). Choose a command category in the Categories list, and then drag the command you want from the Commands list and drop it on the toolbar or menu bar at the desired position.

   You can drop a command on a toolbar, on the menu bar, or on a menu that drops down from a toolbar or the menu bar (the menu will drop down when you drag the command over it).

   To add a custom menu (rather than one of the standard menus in the Commands list), select the New Menu category and then drag the New Menu command to the desired location.

*1. Click the down arrow*

*Check or uncheck commands*

**Figure 14.8** You can remove buttons from a docked toolbar.

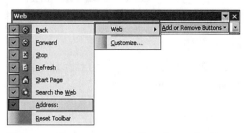

**Figure 14.9** You can remove buttons from a floating toolbar.

**Figure 14.10** The Customize dialog box.

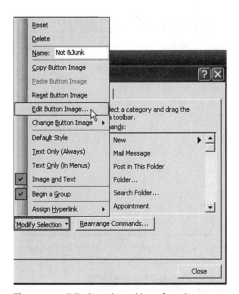

**Figure 14.11** Edit the selected item from its popup menu.

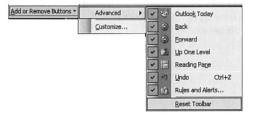

**Figure 14.12** Reset a toolbar to its original state.

**4.** To move a command, leave the Customize dialog box open and drag the command to the new position.

*or*

To copy the command, press Ctrl while you drag.

You can move or copy the command to a different position on the same toolbar or menu bar, or to a different bar.

**5.** To remove a command, leave the Customize dialog box open, drag the command, and drop it anywhere on the screen except on a toolbar or menu bar.

**6.** To modify a command (for example, to change its image), leave the Customize dialog box open, click the command to select it, click the Modify Selection button in the Commands tab, and choose a command from the menu (**Figure 14.11**).

*or*

Leave the Customize dialog box open, right-click the command, and choose a command from the pop-up menu.

**7.** Click the Close button in the Customize dialog box.

## ✔ Tip

- If you've modified a built-in toolbar, you can restore it to its original "factory" configuration by clicking the down arrow (on the end of a docked toolbar or in the upper-left corner of a floating toolbar), clicking Add Or Remove Buttons, *toolbar* (where *toolbar* is the toolbar name), and then choosing Reset Toolbar (**Figure 14.12**).

## To create a custom toolbar:

1. If you want to create a toolbar that you can use in Outlook forms, open any form (except a Note form).

   *or*

   If you want to create a toolbar for use in the main Outlook window, activate that window.

2. Choose Tools > Customize, open the Toolbars tab, and click the New button (**Figure 14.13**).

3. In the New Toolbar dialog box (**Figure 14.14**), type a name for your new toolbar and click the OK button.

   Your new toolbar will initially be devoid of commands. Add the commands you want using the techniques given in the previous section, "To modify a toolbar or the menu bar."

4. To rename or delete a custom toolbar, click on the toolbar name (not on the check box) to select the toolbar and then click the Rename or Delete button.

5. To reset a built-in toolbar that you've modified, click on the toolbar name (not on the check box) to select the toolbar and then click the Reset button.

   The toolbar will be restored to its original "factory" configuration.

6. Click the Close button in the Customize dialog box.

### ✔ Tip

■ Checking or unchecking a toolbar name in the list in the Toolbars tab provides yet another way to show or hide a toolbar.

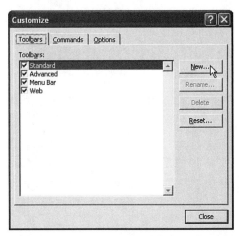

**Figure 14.13** Create a new toolbar with the Toolbars tab.

**Figure 14.14** The New Toolbar dialog box.

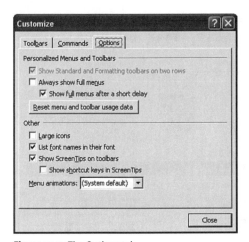

**Figure 14.15** The Options tab.

## To set toolbar and menu options:

1. Choose Tools > Customize, and open the Options tab (**Figure 14.15**).

2. Choose options as desired in the Options tab. For help with a specific option, click the Help button in the upper-right corner and type the help subject.

## ✔ Tip

- The settings you make in the Options tab affect toolbars and menus in both the main Outlook window and in Outlook forms.

# Changing the Office Assistant

You can select a different Outlook Assistant character—for example, Clippit (a paperclip character), F1 (a robot), or Links (a cat). You can also modify the behavior of the Assistant.

### To change the Office Assistant:

1. If the Assistant isn't currently visible, choose Help > Show The Office Assistant.

2. If the Assistant's balloon isn't visible, click the Assistant.

3. Click the Options button in the balloon (**Figure 14.16**).

4. To select a different Assistant character, open the Gallery tab in the Office Assistant dialog box and scroll through the characters by clicking the Next and Back buttons until you find the character you want (**Figure 14.17**).

5. To change the Assistant's behavior, open the Options tab and check the desired options (**Figure 14.18**).

   Unchecking the Use the Office Assistant option disables the Assistant. To reenable it, choose Help > Show The Office Assistant.

6. Click the OK button in the Office Assistant dialog box.

### ✔ Tip

- For instructions on using the Assistant, see "Consulting the Assistant" in Chapter 2.

**Figure 14.16** Set Office Assistant options.

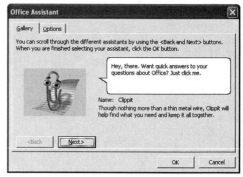

**Figure 14.17** Choose an Office Assistant.

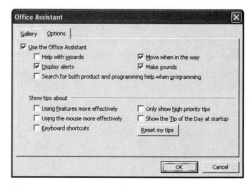

**Figure 14.18** Configure Office Assistant options.

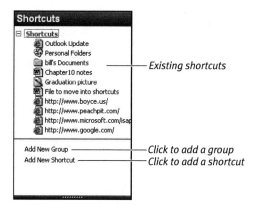

Figure 14.19 Add shortcuts for favorite folders or pages.

*Click on folder*          *Drag folder to the shortcut*

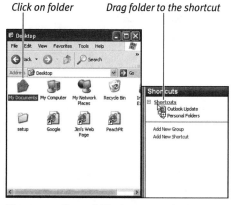

Figure 14.20 Drag a folder to create a shortcut.

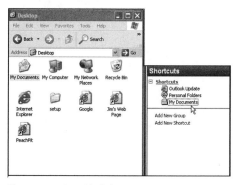

Figure 14.21 An added shortcut.

# Modifying Shortcuts and Groups in the Navigation Pane

The section "How to Get Around in Outlook" in Chapter 2 explained how to use the shortcuts in the Navigation Pane to open Outlook folders as well as file folders. The following sections explain how to modify the Shortcuts Group in the Navigation Pane so that you can streamline your work, organize your information, or accommodate folders you have added or removed (**Figure 14.19**).

### To create a Navigation Pane shortcut to a folder:

1. Click on the Shortcuts button in the Navigation Pane to display the Shortcuts group.

2. Drag the desired folder to the Shortcuts Group (**Figure 14.20**).

   Outlook will add the folder to the Shortcuts Group (**Figure 14.21**). You can drag the folder from Windows Explorer or from a file folder that's opened in Windows.

### To create a Navigation Pane shortcut to a file:

◆ Drag the filename and drop it at the desired position in the Shortcuts Group.

   You can drag the filename from Windows Explorer, or from a file folder that's opened in Windows.

### ✔ Tip

■ For instructions on creating a Navigation Pane shortcut to a Web page (rather than to a folder or to a file), see the section "To create a shortcut to a Web page in your Navigation Pane" in Chapter 13, "Exploring the Web in Outlook."

MODIFYING SHORTCUTS AND GROUPS

## To modify a Navigation Pane shortcut:

**1.** Right-click the shortcut to display the pop-up menu (**Figure 14.22**).

**2.** To rename the shortcut, choose Rename Shortcut.

**3.** To delete the shortcut, choose Delete Shortcut.

### ✔ Tip

■ To move a shortcut, drag it to the desired position. To make a copy of the shortcut, press Ctrl while you drag. Dragging the shortcut over a group and holding the pointer over the top of the group will display the contents of that group.

## To modify Navigation Pane Shortcuts groups:

**1.** Right-click the group you want to work with. Outlook will display a pop-up menu (**Figure 14.23**).

**2.** To remove or rename the group you right-clicked, choose Remove Group or Rename Group.

**3.** Select Move Up in List or Move Down in List to move the shortcut up or down accordingly.

**4.** To create a new group, choose Add New Group.

### ✔ Tips

■ To move shortcuts to files or Web pages from group to group, left-click and drag the shortcut to the desired location in either the original group or another group.

■ Once a folder shortcut is created, it cannot be moved. It can be renamed or deleted only.

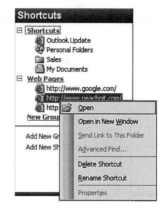

**Figure 14.22** Right-click a shortcut icon.

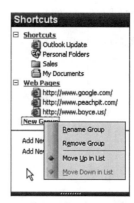

**Figure 14.23** Right-click a group.

■ Hold the Ctrl button while dragging a shortcut to create a copy of the shortcut in another location.

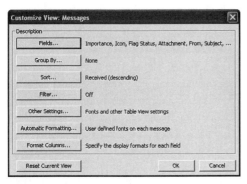

Figure 14.24 The Customize View dialog box.

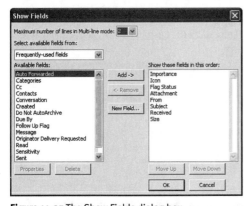

Figure 14.25 The Show Fields dialog box.

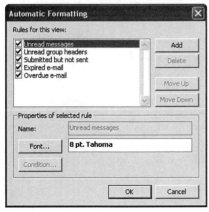

Figure 14.26 The Automatic Formatting dialog box.

# Adjusting Views

Chapter 3, "Working with Outlook Items," explained how to work with the different views of a folder (see the section "Using Different Views"). Chapter 3, in the section "Sorting, Filtering, and Grouping Items," also described how to sort, filter, or group the items in a particular view, which are some of the most common ways to modify a view. In the following sections, you'll learn about some additional ways to modify the current view.

### To customize the current view:

1. Choose View > Arrange By > Current View > Customize Current View.

   Outlook will open the Customize View: "View" box, where "View" is the type of current view. For example, with the Mail group selected, Customize View: Messages box (**Figure 14.24**) is displayed. The buttons available in this dialog box, and their descriptions, depend upon the current folder and view.

2. To change the particular fields that are displayed, or to change the order of the fields, click the Fields button and select your options in the Show Fields dialog box (**Figure 14.25**).

3. To modify the way Outlook formats various types of items—for example, the font and color it uses for unread messages—click the Automatic Formatting button and select your options in the Automatic Formatting dialog box (**Figure 14.26**).

4. To group, sort, or filter the items in the current view, click the Group By, Sort, or Filter button (**Figure 14.24**), and follow the instructions given in "Sorting, Filtering, and Grouping Items" in Chapter 3.

*continues on next page*

ADJUSTING VIEWS

**5.** To change other features of the view, click the Other Settings button and select options in the dialog box that Outlook displays.

The name of the dialog box and its contents depend upon the current view. Chapters 6 through 11 show examples of this dialog box for different folders and views.

## To manage views:

◆ Choose View > Arrange By > Current View > Define Views to open the Custom View Organizer dialog box (**Figure 14.27**), and select the desired options:

   ▲ Create a new custom view, or make a copy of an existing view.

   ▲ Modify any view.

   ▲ Reset any of the built-in views to restore it to its original "factory" settings.

   ▲ Delete or rename a custom view that you've created.

## To format columns in a table view:

**1.** Activate the table view in which you want to format the columns.

**2.** Choose View > Arrange By > Current View > Format Columns to open the Format Columns dialog box (**Figure 14.28**).

**3.** Select the desired options in the dialog box.

## ✔ Tip

■ Changing column width is available only in the single-line layout. In multi-line layout, the columns are resized automatically. Click View > Arrange By > Custom > Other Settings to access line layout settings (**Figure 14.29**).

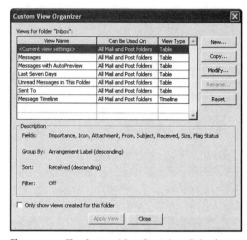

Figure 14.27 The Custom View Organizer dialog box.

Figure 14.28 The Format Columns dialog box.

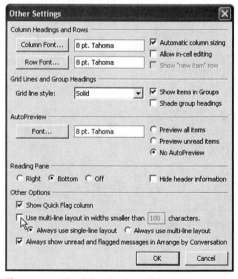

Figure 14.29 The Other Settings dialog box.

**Figure 14.30** A Windows Explorer folder window.

**Figure 14.31** New shortcuts in the Shortcuts pane.

# Working with Folders and Files

Windows provides the Windows Explorer interface for viewing folders and their contents, moving and copying files, deleting files, and opening documents (**Figure 14.30**). If you work with certain folders and files often, you might want to add shortcuts to those folders and files in one or more shortcut groups in Outlook (**Figure 14.31**).

## ✔ Tips

- When you open a folder from a shortcut in the Navigation pane, Outlook opens a standard Windows Explorer window rather than show the folder's contents within Outlook. You can then work with that folder and its contents just as if you had opened it from My Computer, My Documents, or another folder.

- When you click a document shortcut in the Outlook Navigation pane, the document opens in its native program. For example, click a shortcut to a Word document, and Word opens with that document.

### To add a folder or file shortcut to the Navigation Pane:

1. Click the Shortcut button to open Shortcuts in the Navigation pane (**Figure 14.31**).

2. If you want to place the shortcut in a new shortcut group, create the shortcut group as explained earlier in the section, "Modifying Shortcuts and Groups in the Navigation Pane."

3. Open in Windows Explorer the parent folder of the one you want to add to the shortcut group.

   For example, if you are adding C:\download to the shortcut group, open My Computer, then open drive C. Or, open the folder containing the document for which you want to create a shortcut.

4. Position the folder window and Outlook so you can see both the folder (or file) and the shortcut group where you want to create the shortcut (**Figure 14.32**).

5. Click and drag the folder (or file) from the Windows Explorer window to the Navigation Pane, and drop it on the shortcut group under which you want the shortcut created (**Figure 14.33**).

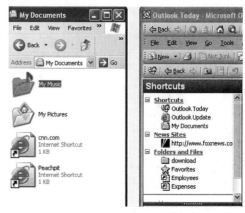

**Figure 14.32** Position the folder and Outlook.

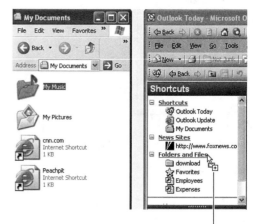

Drag & Drop shortcut on shortcut group

**Figure 14.33** Drag to create shortcut.

# CONFIGURING OUTLOOK

The instructions in this appendix will help you complete some of the more technical tasks that you might encounter when you first set up Outlook. (Basic procedures are discussed in Chapter 1, "Setting Up Outlook 2003.") They will also help you modify the Outlook setup after you've already begun using the program. Here, you'll learn how to:

◆ Create a User Profile

◆ Create and modify a POP3, IMAP, or HTTP Account

◆ Create a Microsoft Exchange Account

◆ Import email settings, messages, or addresses from another email program that you've been using on your computer

◆ Add or remove individual Outlook components, such as Help or Stationery

# Creating a User Profile

An Outlook user profile stores many of the settings for an Outlook session, including your email accounts, address book settings, and other settings that control how Outlook looks and functions for a particular user. You can create and use more than one profile to keep your accounts separate or include all of your accounts in one user profile.

- An Outlook profile is not the same as a Windows user profile, which stores your documents, desktop configuration, and other Windows user information.

- Each Outlook profile has a name. Give yours a name that identifies the contents of the profile (such as Work or Personal), or use your name or logon name as the profile name.

### To create a user profile with the Inbox Setup Wizard:

1. Run the Inbox Setup Wizard in one of the following ways:
   ▲ The Inbox Setup Wizard runs automatically during the initial Outlook setup if a profile hasn't already been created on your computer.

*Mail icon*

**Figure A.1** Double-clicking the Mail icon in the Windows Control Panel.

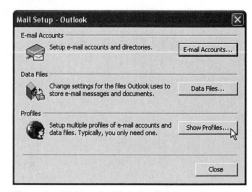

**Figure A.2** Clicking the Show Profiles button.

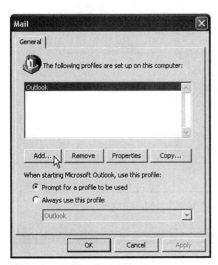

**Figure A.3** Clicking the Add button.

**Figure A.4** The New Profile dialog box.

▲ You can run the Inbox Setup Wizard at any time by double-clicking the Mail icon in your Windows Control Panel folder (**Figure A.1**), clicking the Show Profiles button in the Mail Setup dialog box (**Figure A.2**), and clicking the Add button in the Mail dialog box (**Figure A.3**). If you are using Windows XP in Category View, select User Accounts in your Windows Control Panel first to display the mail icon.

2. In the New Profile dialog box (**Figure A.4**), type the new profile name and click OK to display the E-mail Accounts Wizard. Go to step 2 of "To create a new email account" to set up email accounts for this profile.

# Configuring a POP3, IMAP, or HTTP Account

There are several types of email accounts that you can create. All email accounts follow similar basic creation steps but have tools and options that can vary depending on the type of account selected.

### To create an email account:

1. Choose Tools > E-mail Accounts to display the E-mail Accounts dialog box (**Figure A.5**).

2. Select Add a new email account, and click Next.

3. Select the type of account desired. In this example, select POP3 in the E-mail Accounts dialog box (**Figure A.6**) and click Next.

4. Enter your information into the text boxes. **Figure A.7** displays a completed Internet E-Mail Settings (POP3) dialog box.

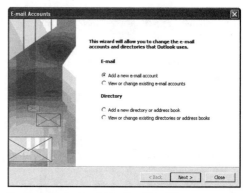

**Figure A.5** Selecting Add a New E-mail Account.

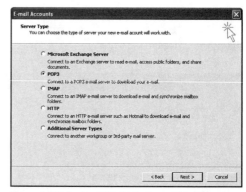

**Figure A.6** Selecting POP3 in the Server Type dialog box.

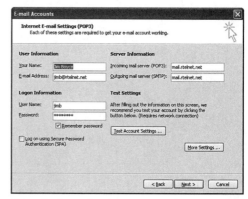

**Figure A.7** A completed Internet E-mail Settings POP3 dialog box.

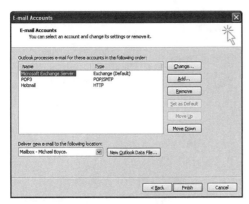

**Figure A.8** E-mail Accounts dialog box.

**Figure A.9** Send as another specified account.

**Figure A.10** The Congratulations screen.

**5.** Click Next to display the accounts that Outlook is configured for, including the one you just set up (**Figure A.8**). Click Change to make changes to existing account settings here. Or select a default email account. All mail is sent from the default account unless specified in a new email message by clicking the Accounts button and selecting another account (**Figure A.9**).

**6.** Click Finish in the Congratulations screen (**Figure A.10**).

## To view or modify settings for an email account:

1. Click Tools > E-mail Accounts.

2. Select View or Change Existing E-mail Accounts.

3. Click Next to display the E-mail Accounts dialog box (**Figure A.8**).

   This dialog box displays your existing accounts and lists them in the order in which they are processed.

4. Select the account you want to modify, and choose Change (**Figure A.11**) to display the Settings dialog box originally displayed in the creation of the account.

5. Make your modifications, and then click Next and Finish to close the E-mail Accounts dialog box.

### ✔ Tips

- POP3 and IMAP email accounts are almost identical to configure. An additional configuration option for a POP3 email account is Test Account Settings (**Figure A.12**). Click this button to have Outlook test your new account to verify that it is configured properly (**Figure A.13**) and to send a test email message to that account.

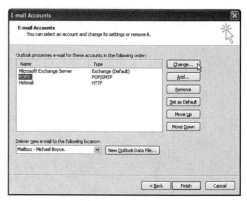

**Figure A.11** Clicking the Change button.

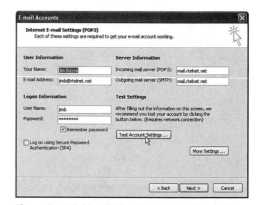

**Figure A.12** Clicking the Test Account Settings button.

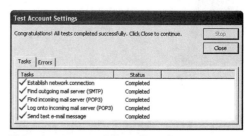

**Figure A.13** A successfully configured account.

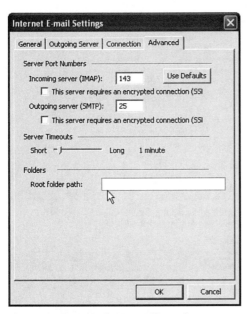

**Figure A.14** Changing the Root Folder path.

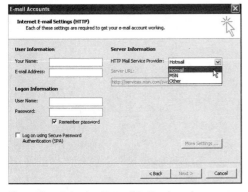

**Figure A.15** Selecting Hotmail in the drop-down menu.

■ You can select the default root folder path of your IMAP mail folder. Follow the steps in the previous "To view or modify settings for an email account" section to get to the Internet E-mail Settings dialog box. Click the More Settings button, and select the Advanced tab. Enter the desired path in the Root Folder Path text box (**Figure A.14**), and click OK to close the E-mail Accounts dialog box.

■ If you create an HTTP email account, you can select Hotmail or MSN from the HTTP Mail Service Provider drop-menu (**Figure A.15**) to automatically configure the Server URL. If you choose Other, you will need to enter the server URL manually.

*continues on next page*

■ Check the box Log on Using Secure Password Authentication (SPA) in the Internet E-mail Settings dialog box (**Figure A.16**) if your email provider uses Secure Password Authentication (such as supported by a server running integrated Active Directory).

■ Click More Settings to display the Internet E-mail Settings dialog box. The General tab (**Figure A.17**) is used to enter information regarding how the account will be referred to in the Mail Account section, such as Jim's mail. In the Other User Information section, specify the Organization (such as company name) if desired.

■ Change the Reply E-mail Account to reflect the account that you want the recipient to send to when they hit the Reply button.

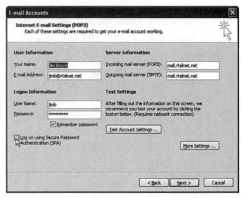

**Figure A.16** Clicking the box Log on Using Secure Password Authentication (SPA).

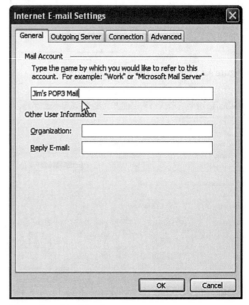

**Figure A.17** Naming the account.

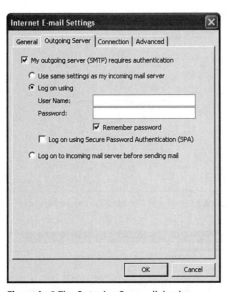

**Figure A.18** The Outgoing Server dialog box.

■ Click The Outgoing Server tab (**Figure A.18**) to configure the account's outgoing authentication. Click the Connection tab (**Figure A.19**) to configure how the email account connects to the server, such as LAN or dial-up. Click the Advanced tab (**Figure A.20**) to change the default Server Port Numbers for incoming and outgoing servers, Server Timeouts, and Delivery settings. In most cases you can leave all of these settings at their default values.

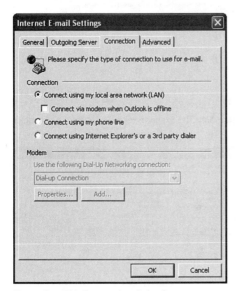

**Figure A.19** The Connection dialog box.

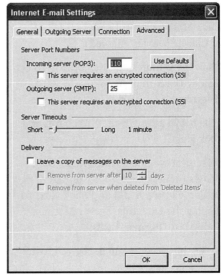

**Figure A.20** The Advanced dialog box.

# Configuring an Exchange Server Account

You can create an account in your profile that connects to a Microsoft Exchange Server. With this configuration, the Outlook folders that contain your mail, such as the Inbox and Sent Items, are stored and managed on the Exchange server.

### To create an Exchange Server account:

1. Navigate to the Control Panel in Windows by clicking Start > Control Panel > User Accounts > Mail (if Category View is enabled). Double-click on the Mail icon to display the Mail Setup dialog box.

   *or*

   Click Start > Control Panel > Mail (if Classic View is enabled).

2. Click the E-mail Accounts button to display the E-mail Accounts Wizard (**Figure A.5**).

3. Select Add a New E-mail Account, and click Next.

4. Select the type of account desired. In this example, select Microsoft Exchange Server (**Figure A.21**) and click Next to display the Exchange Server Settings dialog box (**Figure A.22**).

5. Enter the server name in the Microsoft Exchange Server box.

   This can be the server's NetBIOS name, such as \\SNOOPY, or it might be a fully qualified domain name, such as snoopy.boyce.us.

6. Type the name of the mailbox or email address in the User Name box (**Figure A.23**).

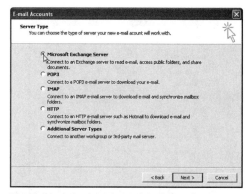

**Figure A.21** Selecting Microsoft Exchange Server.

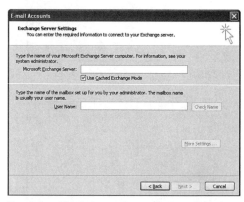

**Figure A.22** The Exchange Server Settings dialog box.

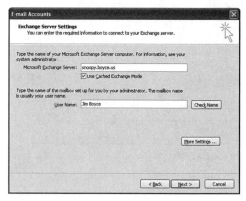

**Figure A.23** Entering the Exchange Server required information.

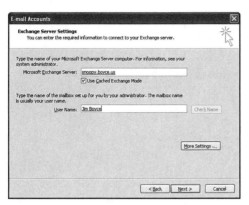

**Figure A.24** Successfully resolved Exchange Server account.

**Figure A.25** Cannot find the account specified.

**Figure A.26** Correcting the Microsoft Exchange Server settings.

**7.** Click the Check Name button to verify the mailbox.

If the account is valid, the User Name box will display the server and account name with an underline (**Figure A.24**).

If the account cannot be found, the messages shown in **Figure A.25** will be displayed. Click OK to display the Microsoft Exchange Server dialog box (**Figure A.26**). Correct the Mailbox name, click Check Name again to locate it, and then click OK.

If the name cannot be resolved, check with your network administrator for the correct mailbox name.

*continues on next page*

**8.** Click Next to display the E-mail Accounts window (**Figure A.27**), which in this example informs you that mail will be delivered to the existing Personal Folder.

**9.** If you have a POP3 account and want messages from that account to be delivered to your Exchange Server mailbox, select your mailbox from the Deliver New E-mail to the Following Location drop-down list.

## ✔ Tips

■ If Exchange Server is your only mail account, all of your mail will be delivered to your Exchange Server mailbox. If you have a POP3 account, however, and that POP3 account has its own set of Personal Folders, you can configure the account to deliver your Exchange Server mail to your PST. Select the Personal Folders from the drop-down list labeled Deliver New E-mail to the Following Location. When you check your email, Outlook downloads your mail from the Exchange Server and places it in your Personal Folders. If Exchange Server is your main mailbox, you should deliver mail to Exchange Server rather than to a set of personal folders.

■ If you have configured the Exchange Server account as the location for new mail delivery, mail that comes in to your POP3 account is moved to your Exchange Server mailbox. Mail from IMAP and HTTP accounts is delivered to the Personal Folders of these accounts, however. If you want everything to be delivered to your Exchange Server mailbox, create a rule that copies messages from the IMAP and HTTP accounts to your Exchange Server Inbox.

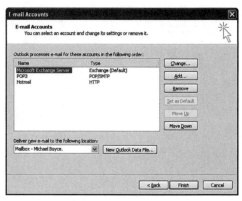

**Figure A.27** The E-mail Accounts window.

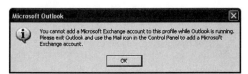

**Figure A.28** Close Outlook before creating an Exchange account.

■ If Outlook is running when you attempt to create a Microsoft Exchange Server account, you will be prompted to close Outlook first (**Figure A.28**). Click OK, close Outlook, and try again.

■ It's a good idea to configure Outlook to deliver your mail to your Exchange Server mailbox rather than a local PST, because placing the mail in the Exchange Server mailbox makes it available from Outlook Web Access and makes it available for the Exchange Server administrator to back up. You can archive messages as needed to a set of local personal folders to manage the size of your Exchange Server mailbox.

CONFIGURING AN EXCHANGE SERVER ACCOUNT

# Using Multiple Profiles

You might want to create more than one user profile. For example, if several people use Outlook on a single computer, each person can have a separate profile with personalized settings. Or, you might want to have one profile for your business settings and another for your personal settings.

### To set up several profiles:

1. Create one or more additional profiles following the directions that were given in the section "To create a user profile with the Inbox Setup Wizard."

2. Choose Start > Control Panel, select the Mail icon, and click the Show Profiles button (**Figure A.29**) to display the Mail dialog box.

3. Select either of the following two options in the Startup settings area:

   ▲ Prompt for a Profile to be Used causes Outlook to prompt you for the profile it will use, each time you start the program.

   ▲ Always Use this Profile causes Outlook—each time you start the program—to automatically use the profile you select in the adjoining list box.

### ✔ Tip

■ You can work with your profiles by double-clicking the Mail icon in the Windows Control Panel folder, and then clicking the Show Profiles button to open the Mail dialog box (**Figure A.3**). Then, by selecting a profile and clicking the appropriate button, you can remove, change properties, or make a copy of the profile. To specify the default profile, select a profile from the drop-down list labeled When Starting Microsoft Outlook Use This Profile.

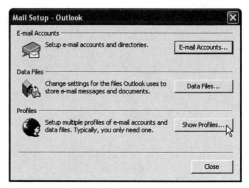

**Figure A.29** Clicking the Show Profiles button.

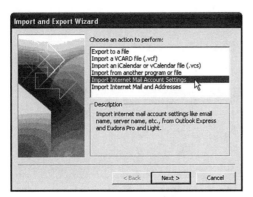

**Figure A.30** Selecting Import Internet Mail Account Settings.

# Importing Settings or Data from Another Email Program

As explained in Chapter 1, during initial Outlook setup, you might be given the opportunity to import the email messages, stored addresses, and settings from another email program that is already installed on your computer (that is, to "upgrade" that program). You can also do this at any time after Outlook has been set up. The programs you can upgrade include Qualcomm Eudora Pro, Eudora Light, and Microsoft Outlook Express.

### To import settings or mail and addresses from another email program:

1. Choose File > Import And Export.

2. In the first Import And Export Wizard dialog box (**Figure A.30**), select the Import Internet Mail Account Settings list item to import settings from another email program.

   *or*

   Select the Import Internet Mail and Addresses item to import messages and stored addresses from another email program.

3. Click the Next button.

   If Outlook finds one or more email programs it can upgrade installed on your computer, it prompts you for further information.

4. Select the program you want to import from and supply the other requested information.

# Adding or Removing Outlook Components

If you're missing an Outlook feature you require, you might need to install an additional Outlook program component. You might also want to uninstall a program component that you never use.

## To install or uninstall Outlook components:

1. Quit Outlook and any other Office application that is running.

2. Double-click the Add or Remove Programs icon in your Windows Control Panel (**Figure A.31**).

3. In the Currently Installed Programs window, select the name of the Microsoft product that Outlook came with (for example, Microsoft Outlook 2003 Professional Edition, as shown in **Figure A.32**) and click the Change button.

4. Select Add or Remove Features in the Microsoft Office 2003 Setup window (**Figure A.33**) for adding or removing Outlook program features, and follow the instructions that are displayed.

## ✔ Tip

■ If you are having problems with Outlook, you can choose Reinstall or Repair in the Microsoft Office 2003 Setup window, or choose to uninstall Outlook completely.

**Figure A.31** Double-clicking the Add or Remove Programs icon.

**Figure A.32** Clicking the Change button.

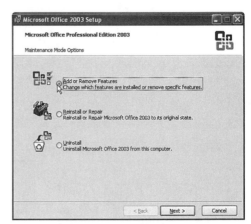

**Figure A.33** Selecting Add or Remove Features.

# INDEX

## G

## U-V

## W-Z

INDEX

www.informit.com

## YOUR GUIDE TO IT REFERENCE

**New Riders** has partnered with **InformIT.com** to bring technical information to your desktop. Drawing from New Riders authors and reviewers to provide additional information on topics of interest to you, **InformIT.com** provides free, in-depth information you won't find anywhere else.

### Articles

Keep your edge with thousands of free articles, in-depth features, interviews, and IT reference recommendations— all written by experts you know and trust.

### Online Books

Answers in an instant from **InformIT Online Books'** 600+ fully searchable online books.

POWERED BY

**Safari**

### Catalog

Review online sample chapters, author biographies, and customer rankings and choose exactly the right book from a selection of over 5,000 titles.

**New Riders**

www.newriders.com